# Assertive

A working woman's guide to standing up for
nication and assertiveness without feeling guilty, yelling, or people pleasing.

By Natalie White

Table of Contents

Introduction 1

Chapter 1: Myths and Misconceptions 6

Chapter 2: The Benefits of Assertive Communication 11

Chapter 3: Other Communication Styles 16

Chapter 4: Assertive Communication Skills 32

Chapter 5: Setting Boundaries 46

Chapter 6: Communicating In An Emotional State 56

Chapter 7: Frequently Asked Questions (FAQ) 67

Chapter 8: Traps That You May Fall Into When Communicating Assertively 74

Chapter 9: What Should You Do When You Slip up? 83

Chapter 10: Assertive Communication for Different Settings 86

Chapter 11: Sample Scripts for Assertive Communication 92

Conclusion 99

Thank You From Story Ninjas 102

About Story Ninjas 103

About The Author 105

Introduction

There are many times the most appropriate response to a request is no. Yet, if you are agreeable by nature (or by necessity), it can be a struggle to politely decline. Even if the request is ludicrous. Even if you're quadruple booked. Even if the thought of sitting in an hour-long meeting (that should've been an email) is more appealing than completing the request. You. still. can't. say. NO!

You don't want to be mean! You're a good person. You're nice...maybe too nice.

What if I told you: *Sometimes when you think you're being nice, you are actually just trying to manage/control the situation?*

SPOILER: You probably learned this people pleasing strategy as a child and/or through social conditioning.

You didn't know at the time that the "being nice" action doesn't always have an equal and opposite reaction. Maybe you just felt some bitterness and resentment later but shamed yourself with "I just can't be mean like that" or "I should've known better". Don't worry I'll address how being nice is a way to control the reactions of others and the interaction.

In this book I'm going to show you that the social convention of "nice" is often unhelpful. I will introduce compassion, empathy, respect and kindness in the form of assertive communication. This type of communication has many of the benefits of being nice without the bitterness and resentment that comes with self-betrayal.

This book is specifically written for the unique concerns of a working woman who identifies as "nice" or "agreeable". However, I firmly believe Assertive communication is for everyone: introverts, extroverts, ambiverts, women or men, stay-at-home or working women, codependent or dependent, leaders or followers. Everyone.

Welcome to *Assertive & Kind!* This book is for you if:

- You are a people pleaser, and you feel like it has begun to impact your life in negative ways. For example, you're too nice: you always say "yes" when you want to say "no," and then you feel bitter.

- After being too nice for too long, you have trouble communicating your thoughts, feelings, and needs without people thinking that you are yelling or being aggressive.

Many of us can think of times when we knew we should have spoken up, but we didn't, or when we felt like we were being taken advantage of, but we just can't say no. After the fact, we kick ourselves, thinking: "If only I would have said something!"

What is Communication?

In this section, we will learn about communication in a general sense before delving into assertive communication throughout the rest of this book. Communication, in its most basic form, is a way of exchanging information with others. There are many different ways that humans can communicate with each other. With the advent of technology, additional forms of communication have come about.

Communication is not only an important part of our relationships but also our day-to-day life. You will often communicate with people in some way without even having a relationship with them. For example, when you go to the store, you will communicate with the cashier. You may also give them a nod or a look at someone else in their car as a form of communication. Communication has been key to interpersonal connections long before the modern languages we know and use now came about. Communicating effectively is useful for interactions in your workplace, in your home and family life, in your leisure activities, and in your everyday interactions as you move through the world alongside other people.

What is Assertive Communication?

Assertive communication is a communication style that involves directly expressing yourself without resorting to either a passive or an aggressive extreme. This style of communication is extremely effective at minimizing conflict and getting your points across clearly.

Throughout this book, we will learn about what assertive communication entails, how you can use it, and some of its many benefits. This book will help you to express yourself in the most effective way possible. Continue reading to change your communication style and your life for good!

Who Should Read This Book?

- Anyone who wants to improve their personal relationships

- Anyone who wants to improve their professional relationships

- Anyone who wants to communicate more effectively

- Anyone serious about making a change in their life

- Anyone willing to put in the work to improve themselves
- Anyone who is done being a doormat!
- Anyone who is done being angry and yelling!
- Anyone who wants to be heard and understood
- Anyone brave enough to state their intentions clearly, respectfully, and openly

This book will help you if you are a person who needs to increase your level of assertiveness, improve your communication skills, deal with conflict in a better way, improve your level of confidence and be a better leader. In this book, you will learn how to improve all of these skills and more!

Who Should NOT Read This Book?

- Anyone who wants to avoid all of their problems
- Anyone who isn't willing to see the part they play in their problems
- Anyone who wants to argue with people
- Anyone who isn't open-minded
- Anyone who isn't willing to put in the work
- Anyone who over-identifies with their current communication style and believes it is an integral part of their personality. For example, someone who thinks "I'm just a passive person," or "I'm passive aggressive," "I've always been like this; it's just the way I am."

The purpose of this book is to serve as a guide that will help you understand what assertiveness is and how you can become more assertive in your own life. Using practical exercises and techniques will teach you how to say yes to what you need, ask for what you want and need, and say no to what you don't want. It will teach you to do this in a way that's confident, calm, and respectful.

This book will also serve as a guide to increasing self-confidence. By reading this book and learning these things, you will find that your life improves in several ways, including giving you more control over your life, improving your communication skills and interpersonal skills, and making you more successful in your personal and work life.

By the end of this book, you will be well equipped to change your life for the better in numerous ways. This book will have you wondering how you ever lived without this information.

Now that you understand a little bit about what assertive communication is and who should read this book, we will spend some time delving into the assertive communication style and how it will serve you. To begin, we will learn about some common myths associated with assertive communication. There is no better time than now to change the parts of yourself that you wish were different, so don't wait, read on!

Chapter 1: Myths and Misconceptions

First, we will discuss what it means to be assertive and some myths and misconceptions related to assertiveness so that you can get a better idea of what exactly it means. First, making sure that you understand assertiveness will help you understand what benefits can come from employing an assertive communication style.

What is a Communication Style?

A communication style is a term used to describe the ways that people communicate with each other. There are four main styles of communication. They are as follows;

- Passive communication style
- Passive-aggressive communication style
- Assertive communication style
- Aggressive communication style

There are various things that set different communication styles apart from each other, which we will learn later in this book.

What Does it Mean to be Assertive?

Assertiveness is being able to use effective communication as well as negotiation to express your personal needs and boundaries when interacting with other people. Assertive Communication skills are valuable both in personal and work or professional life.

What it DOESN'T Mean to be Assertive.

Here is a list of things that are NOT assertive communication.

- Assertive communication is not shutting down others in a conversation so they can't respond.

- Assertive communication is not asking people to please do things exactly as you describe.

- Assertive communication does not involve speaking over people.

- Assertive communication is not saying yes when you mean no and allowing others to walk all over you.

Myths About an Assertive Communication Style

1. Being Assertive is a Trait That you are Born With or Without.

Some people think that being assertive is something that you either have or do not have- that you are born with or without, similar to height or the color of your eyes.

This belief is untrue, however. Being assertive is a skill and not an innate characteristic. What does this mean? As I am sure you can imagine, a skill is something that you can learn and develop. This is the opposite of an innate characteristic, which is something that you are born with. Examples of this can be the color of your eyes, as mentioned, or certain aspects of your personality, such as a disagreeable disposition.

Skills are things that you can study, practice, and improve upon. Skills are things like communication or cooking. On the other hand, a characteristic is something that you possess that you do not have much control over. You can wear colored contacts to change the color of your eyes but at the end of the day your eyes are the color they are.

The primary vehicle for skill building is mindset. The type of mindset that you employ has a very large impact on your life and your growth as a person. The 'growth mindset' is a term that was coined by Carol Dweck, who is a renowned professor at multiple universities, including Columbia University, Harvard University, and the University of Illinois. Her research with Angela Lee Duckworth stated that intelligence is not a key indicator of success. In fact, they believed that success depends on whether or not a person has a growth mindset. A 'growth mindset' is a term for the belief that skills can be developed through hard work and perseverance (and often multiple failures). A 'fixed mindset' is the exact opposite, intelligence and skills are fixed traits and that cannot be changed at all... ever. People of this mindset believe they have what they have, and that's all.

Knowing your communication style can be developed is empowering and hopeful. If you struggle with confidence and assertiveness, understanding that these skills can be learned and honed over time means that you don't have to keep struggling. By picking up this book, you are already taking the first steps involved in changing your life by becoming a more confident and more assertive person. In this book we will discuss exactly how you can make these changes in your life.

1. Being Aggressive or Being Passive Protects You From Getting Hurt.

One of the main reasons that people struggle with being assertive is they are trying to protect themselves. A person may not even realize that they are avoiding assertiveness to protect themselves. A person may genuinely want to be more assertive, but they avoid assertiveness to feel secure and think they are in control of their life (and others' reactions). They think they are in control because passive communication works as a short term solution to avoid conflict. It is a defense mechanism.

Defense mechanisms are attempts to avoid getting hurt or minimize the risk of getting hurt. A person uses these to protect themselves from real or perceived danger. This can include acting in a submissive manner, shutting down (silencing yourself), blaming, and keeping physical and emotional distance between yourself and others. Fear is a very common reason that people lack assertiveness, and it is something that we will address heavily in this book.

There could be many reasons behind this effort to avoid getting hurt. The most common reasons actually begin in childhood, believe it or not. Our upbringing and childhood experiences typically play a huge role in how you interact as an adult. Did you grow up in a strict family who barely ever gave you praise? Were you always overshadowed by a more successful sibling? Did you grow up in a family where nobody was ever around, and you were left to fend for yourself?

Many people experience multiple difficulties like these in childhood and much worse. These experiences are not a sentence of eternal brokenness. Through therapy they move from victims of their past to survivor to thriving because of the effort they put in to heal. If you don't have any of these experiences but have the resources to go to therapy, it's still worth your time.

If you have experienced multiple adverse experiences like these as a child or adult including but not limited to a traumatic event, reach out to a mental health professional first. This book is NOT a replacement for therapy. Frankly, I could write another book on the topic of avoiding underlying issues by reading self-help.

Recap and Action Items

Did you learn anything in this chapter that surprised you? Did this chapter dispel any myths or preconceived opinions that you had about what assertive communication means? Write them down so that you can remind yourself as you read through this book.

Chapter 2: The Benefits of Assertive Communication

In this chapter, we will look at the many benefits of assertive communication so that you can get an idea of what you can expect to gain by employing assertive communication.

The Benefits

There are numerous benefits to assertiveness, many of which you are likely aware of, or you would not have opened this book in the first place. This section will look at some of the most valuable benefits of being an assertive person.

- Being assertive allows you to communicate confidently and clearly.

- Being assertive allows you to practice self-respect by setting boundaries and sticking to them.

- Being assertive allows you to deal with conflict in your personal and professional lives in the most effective and mature manner.

- Being assertive allows you to share your ideas and thoughts clearly and calmly, which will command attention and respect.

- Being assertive allows you to feel comfortable and confident saying "no."

- Being assertive helps you meet your needs.

- Being assertive helps you to effectively provide constructive feedback.

- Being assertive improves your interpersonal skills.

- Being assertive helps you build confidence in yourself, your decisions and ideas.

- Being assertive helps you prioritize your time and energy, reducing stress levels.

- Being assertive improves the way you see yourself and builds confidence.

- Being assertive improves your negotiating skills.

- Being assertive helps you to remain calm under pressure.

The Relationship Between Assertive Communication and Self-Confidence and Self-Worth

When people have a healthy level of self-confidence, they typically have a positive view of themselves. They believe in their capabilities to achieve goals and do not spend a lot of time dwelling on failure. They are not afraid to ask for help from others to help them reach their goals. They can also be assertive and say "no" to situations or requests that they do not want to do.

A healthy level of confidence is built through practice. The overconfident person lacks experience to back up their rhetoric. They seem to have the experience and knowledge, but when push comes to shove they make rookie mistakes. While the person who lacks confidence has the experience but is afraid to put it into practice. Others count on them to perform at the level of their experience; however, due to fear of failure they underperform and usually disappoint everyone including themselves. This experience seems to validate the belief that they are indeed, "not good enough." However, a person with healthy self-confidence knows their abilities and leverages their experience to take appropriate risks with the humility to ask for help when necessary.

Having a healthy level of self-confidence helps increase assertiveness because you believe in what you are saying and doing. If you believe that you need or want something, you won't spend time dwelling on whether you think other people think it is true; you will just ask for it. Those who have low self-confidence typically suffer because they are unable to ask for what they need or want. Afraid of being judged or rejected, they view asking for anything as a sign of weakness. On the flip side, somebody with a healthy level of self-confidence typically isn't afraid of that because the reward of fulfilling their need is worth the risk of being judged or rejected (even multiple times). They even perceive failure and rejection as necessary to reach their goals. Healthy self-confidence comes from loving and respecting yourself enough to express your needs, despite the possibility of rejection.

Now, you may be wondering why I'm not addressing self-esteem. If you're a millennial, you grew up with the idea that high self-esteem leads to success. Self-esteem is a person's perception of their value. If you want to be successful, just view yourself as a high value person. As a society, we are starting to see a group of people who are bitter and disappointed because of this. They expected certain outcomes (benefits) based on their perception of themselves rather than their actions. The unfortunate reality is that high levels of self-esteem without lived experience often leads to entitlement.

I want to be very clear about the value of a person. There is a difference between self-esteem and self-worth. Every person has inherent value and is worthy of existing in this world. That is self worth. The chances of you (just as you are) being born are nothing short of a miracle. You are worthy of existing and you didn't need to do anything to earn your worthiness, and you can't do anything to decrease worthiness.

You are not a failure, you are a person who has tried and failed.

You can build self confidence through practice and challenging yourself to got outside of your comfort zone. Just like a person lifting weights.

Make no mistake, we live in a world that has a hierarchy and favors certain traits and outcomes. However, where you land is this hierarchy is unrelated to your inherent value as a human being. If your goal is to improve your position in society, then develop your skills and abilities through experience.

While self-confidence and assertiveness are related, self-confidence may not be available to you right now because of your history and lack of experience. Throughout this book, you will see how self-confidence and assertiveness play into one another and how they come together in many different situations.

Recap and Action Items

In this chapter, we learned about the benefits of using an assertive communication style and the relationship that this communication style has to a person's self-confidence and self-worth.

Try to think about your level of self-confidence. Is it low, high, or very high? If it is low or very high, think of ways to level it out and bring it to a healthy level. Try the exercise below to help you.

Think of a few of your roles, traits, skills or abilities and a quick description of how you would like to develop them. It is most helpful to write them down, for clarity.

For example, I am a mother. A good mom is one that loves and cares for her children. I would like to develop a closer relationship with my children. To do this, I will focus on improving my work/life balance and fully show up for my children. I will ask for help when I'm exhausted and focus my efforts on creating quality time rather than increasing quantity. I will do this by having a "date night" with each child, reading 2 bedtime stories with my 4 year old every night and inviting my 10 year old to cook dinner with me.

Now, you are ready to post the action items. Start small. The premise here is to build confidence through actions and possibly experience disappointment. Showing up is all that's required. The only rule is *shame doesn't belong here.*

Chapter 3: Other Communication Styles

We have discussed assertive communication thus far, but in this chapter, we will learn about the other communication styles that exist. This helps you determine which style you currently use and which style is beneficial for specific situations. Clearly by the title of this book, I think there is enough evidence to indicate Assertive Communication is the most effective communication for MOST scenarios.

It is also important to note that communication styles, verbal and nonverbal cues vary widely across different cultures. For example, silence can be a sign of respect in one culture and a sign of irritation in another. Eye contact is respectful to some cultures but comes off as aggressive to others. A good rule of thumb is to approach interactions with curiosity, rather than judgement and expect to learn by failing.

Different Types of Communication

Communication is not only an important part of our relationships but also our day-to-day life. You can communicate with people and not even have a relationship with them.

For example, when you go to the store, you communicate with the cashier. You may also give a nod or a look or a finger to a person in their car as a form of communication.

Communication is the key to interpersonal connection. Being able to communicate effectively is useful for interactions in your workplace, in your home and family life, in your leisure activities, and in your everyday interactions as you move through the world alongside other people. These different scenarios involving communication include both verbal and nonverbal communication. We will look at each of these in more detail below.

Verbal Communication

Everybody can use basic communication- this propensity for verbal communication is something that humans are born with, which is why we can learn languages with such ease as babies. This does not mean, however, that everybody can communicate effectively or with skill. While the ability to communicate is something that we are born with, effective communication is a skill that must be learned.

The most basic level of verbal communication involves speaking simple words and phrases and expressing basic needs (such as being hungry or having to go to the bathroom). Basic communication also includes hearing what another person is saying to you and understanding what it means.

Within the umbrella of verbal communication, there are different types. We will look at these types in more detail now. The four types of verbal communication include; intrapersonal communication, interpersonal communication, small group communication, and public communication.

- Intrapersonal Communication

Intrapersonal communication is a type of communication that only involves oneself. This type of communication comes in the form of thoughts. This type of communication likely goes on all of the time within your mind but is often done without your conscious awareness of the fact that it is a type of communication. We use this type of communication while making decisions about our actions or thinking about concepts. We often switch back and forth between the listener and the speaker during this type of communication as we are, in a way, bouncing ideas off of ourselves. This type of communication can remain intrapersonal if not shared with others, or it can become the next type of communication if we then decide to verbalize it with others.

- Interpersonal Communication (one-on-one)

The next type of communication is called interpersonal or one-on-one communication. While the words intrapersonal and interpersonal seem similar at first glance, their meaning is different. One-on-one communication means communication between two people. This type is what happens when we are in a group of two, having a one-on-one interaction. In this type of communication, both people are the listener and the speaker, and they will switch back and forth between roles depending on who is speaking.

- Small-Group Communication

Small group communication is a type of interpersonal communication when there are more than two people involved in the interaction. In this type of communication, the group is small enough that the conversation is still intimate. In this case, the conversation is small enough that all people are participating in it together, and each person is able to interact with all others. This type of communication can happen in a small group of friends, in a family, or in a meeting in the workplace. Sometimes, in these interactions, the information is not transmitted easily to every member of this small group, and misunderstandings can result in much more than interpersonal interactions.

- Public Communication

Public communication is the final type of verbal communication. This typically involves one person speaking to a large group of people. This type is not considered a conversation because usually, only one person will be the speaker, and everyone else will be the listeners. This happens when someone is giving a talk to a group of people, such as in a university lecture or during an election. In this case, only one person is able to share their thoughts and opinions, unlike interpersonal and small group communications, which involve conversations between people.

NONVERBAL COMMUNICATION

Communication can be taken much further than the basics, as there are many subtle ways that people communicate without saying a single word. Being able to pick up on these silent forms of communication while interacting with someone is what differentiates basic communication from effective and intelligent communication. This type of communication is called nonverbal communication.

What exactly do I mean when I say nonverbal communication? I mean the wide variety of ways that people communicate without using words. This involves things that people do, which sends messages about how they think and feel.

This type of physical communication can be either conscious or unconscious, meaning that a person may not even know that they have shared their thoughts, feelings, or opinions with others without using their words.

Humans are quite selective about what they choose to share with others. They choose when and whom to share information with, but their bodies sometimes tell a different story. It is important to understand this concept and recognize what messages you may be sending unconsciously. You can then learn to read and pick up on the messages that others may be unconsciously sending you. Below we will look at two examples of nonverbal communication.

- Vocal Dynamics

One example of nonverbal communication is the use of vocal dynamics. Vocal Communication may seem similar to verbal communication; however, there is a lot more to a sentence than the words it contains. The way that someone delivers a sentence is much more telling than the words it contains. For example, the inclusion of a pause or a drawn-out word and even complete silence can tell you about a person's internal state.

If a person becomes suddenly silent, they may be offended by the topic of conversation or by something that was said. If the person avoids silence at all costs, they are likely a nervous or anxious person who is uncomfortable with a silent moment or two. The tone of voice and volume play a huge part in this as well.

If you didn't understand a word that someone was saying but could read their verbal communication cues, you would be able to tell a lot about what they were trying to convey. Like facial expressions, this is another type of nonverbal communication that we learn when we are very young. We can tell the difference between a happy and an angry sentence even before we have a full vocabulary to use and understand the meaning of the sentence.

The volume of a person's voice can also indicate traits of their personality or their current state. If they are speaking very quietly, they are probably shy or nervous, while a loud volume can mean that they are angry or excited. A great example of the tone of a person's voice demonstrating more than what their words are saying is sarcasm. When we are using sarcasm, our voice's tone is exactly the opposite of what we are saying.

The message we are trying to convey is not evident in the words we are saying but rather in the tone in which we are saying them. If someone misunderstood our tone, they would be very confused. If we say, "I loved waiting in line for four hours," the tone we say it with indicates that we actually mean exactly the opposite.

- Body Language

Body language is a fairly broad term and can include various forms of nonverbal communication, such as hand gestures and facial expressions, but also includes touch and head movements. Body language can be conscious or unconscious. Most of us are very familiar with conscious body language as we more than likely use this as a form of communication on a regular basis.

An example of a conscious display of body language is hand signals. These vary between cultures and regions of the world, but every culture has some. They may change with changes in pop culture, or they may be long-standing such as the thumbs up in North America. These hand signals are a form of body language that we use to convey specific messages to others. Another example is a handshake. A handshake is a nonverbal way of saying that you are welcoming someone to contact you and is a friendly greeting upon meeting someone new.

An example of body language that can be both conscious and unconscious is facial expressions. There are many facial expressions that we consciously make in order to convey messages to people. Facial expressions can convey anger, sadness, or happiness. Humans often make these facial expressions to tell others how they feel without speaking. Unconscious facial expressions happen when we unintentionally communicate with our facial expressions, as in the unfortunate case of RBF (resting B**** face). Microexpressions are also unconscious facial expressions that last less than a second but indicate our true emotional reactions.

These are just two examples of the nonverbal communication that humans exhibit. Some other examples include hand signals, facial expressions, and eye contact.

Nonverbal communication and verbal communication go hand-in-hand, and we must understand both to be able to improve our communication skills and choose the appropriate communication style. Below, we will learn about the four different communication styles that exist.

THE 4 COMMUNICATION Styles & When To Use Them

We will now do a self-examination in order to determine what type of communicator we use most often. Communication comes in many different forms, but in this case, we will look at different verbal communication styles. As a reminder, we use a combination of all of these styles but can usually pin ourselves down to one style the majority of the time.

Understanding the way we communicate can help us express our thoughts and ideas more effectively. Understanding the way others communicate helps us receive and understand others' thoughts and ideas. We will examine the four styles of verbal communication and identify when it's most effective to use them. It is important to note that aside from the clear bias we have toward Assertive Communication (as indicated in the title of this book) other communication styles have their place. Yes, even aggressive communication.

Aggressive Communication Style

THE FIRST COMMUNICATION style we will explore is the Aggressive Communication Style. This communication style is born out of a place of fear. This person fears they will not be heard or understood, and therefore they enter into interaction or conversation with a loud volume and an urgency. If the situation is not urgent, however, it shows an attitude of entitlement and lack of respect for another person.

Aggressive Communicators approach the conversation with a wide stance and a confrontational posture. They shout or talk over others and force their point of view. This style of communication is meant for emergencies, often to indicate danger. If communication styles were tools, aggressive communication is the hammer. When used to bludgeon listeners it can often end up having the exact effect the communicator is trying to avoid. People ignore the content because they are distracted by the way that it has been conveyed. When people are faced with an aggressive communication style, they tend to have survival responses like fight, flight or freeze. They become defensive and closed-off, unwilling to engage much further in the interaction.

The person who uses aggressive communication may lack empathy, may not know how to manage their anger or resentments, may have grown up with this style modeled to them, may want to feel superior because of insecurities, may have had great success with this style in their past, or anything in between. Notice that none of these reasons start with "you are ..." The listener is not the reason the speaker chooses his personal communication style. Other people's communication and subsequent reactions are their responsibility not yours.

Other times you'll see aggressive communication is with passive and passive aggressive communicators who are either starting their journey to assertive communication OR have built up resentment. The aggressive communicator fear is: not being heard. If you are a passive communicator your perspective can't be heard because you don't share it. If you are a passive aggressive communicator your perspective was probably misunderstood. When these two styles use aggressive communication, the fall-out is usually guilt and shame.

Aggressive communication often comes with negative consequences. I know it's hard to believe but there is a time and place for this communication style - short term. This communication style is best suited for an emergency situation. When someone is about to get hit by a car, it would not be effective to say, "I feel panic right now because I value human life and yours is about to be taken by that car. Please step out of the way. If you choose not to move, you may be badly injured or die." You would not passively say "I don't really care but can you please step out of the way of the car if you want?" You would not passive aggressively say "why don't you just stand there so you can get hit by a car?"

You would LOUDLY talk over others and say RUN! or MOVE! or GET OUT OF THE WAY! or CAR! or even HEY! There is no time for "please", social conventions, or even full sentences. Yelling "get out of the way" is rude, unless that person is about to be hit by a moving vehicle.

For my aggressive communicators: those emergencies don't happen as often as you think, use sparingly or risk pushing people away.

Passive Communication Style

THE SECOND IS THE PASSIVE Communication Style. This type of communicator prefers to avoid conflict at all costs. They would rather please people than make their opinion known. Passive communicators will often say they are "too nice" while subconsciously attempting to control the other person's response through acquiesce. After all, who would create conflict with someone who agrees with and does everything they say?

They are easily swayed, struggle to make even simple decisions, and speak with a very low volume. They attempt to shrink themselves down using their body language with hunched shoulders and crossed arms.

They think their opinions are not valid and rarely express them. Misunderstandings are rampant with this communication style.

Their operating system is also fear, but instead of fight, they choose flight. They often personalize events and are easily offended. Other people will approach this type of communicator in an exasperated manner as they feel that they have to walk on eggshells in an effort to preserve the person's feelings.

The person who uses passive communication may have experienced a difficult childhood where if they spoke up there was a risk of violence, may not be able to identify their own needs, may have grown up with this style modeled to them, may value comfort over convenience, may have high levels of anxiety, or anything in between. Again, none of these reasons start with "you are ..." Other people's communication and subsequent reactions are their responsibility not yours.

It can be used as an effective short term strategy when there is a real risk of escalation to violence. It is also an effective strategy when listening is the primary objective to the conversation. It's not necessary to share your perspective in every conversation, particularly if you are inexperienced or uneducated in the topic. Long term use of this style builds resentment in both the person using it and others.

Passive-Aggressive Communication Style

THE NEXT IS THE PASSIVE-Aggressive Communication Style. It is the combination of both of the previous two styles of communication. These types of communicators initially show one type of attitude on the outside, that their words do not match. They use passive, self-shrinking body language, therefore, appearing to be passive and non-confrontational on the outside while communicating with their words in an aggressive manner.

They tend to speak in an aggressive manner to indirectly make a point but act out passively in front of the person. Their words are of an aggressive nature, but they deliver them in a passive style. They will use a low volume and a gentle tone while saying something that is likely to cause confrontation or to make someone angry. Often communication like this is followed up with the "silent treatment", gossip, and subtle sabotaging of another's efforts while public praising them.

People tend to become frustrated when dealing with this type of communicator because there is a lot of close attention that needs to be paid to figure out what they are trying to say. This communicator's actions don't match their words and struggle to develop trusting relationships because of this. It is often used by people who wish to be of an aggressive style but who are afraid to speak out in such a way.

THE PERSON WHO USES passive aggressive communication may have experienced a difficult childhood, may feel powerless, may value comfort over convenience, may have high levels of anxiety, or anything in between. Again, none of these reasons start with "you are ..." Other people's communication and subsequent reactions are their responsibility not yours.

USED INTENTIONALLY, this style can be a fun way to joke with friends; we haven't come up with a scenario where this communication style is most effective. The unfortunate reality is that passive aggressive communication is one of the most frequently used and socially acceptable ways of expressing anger. This is especially true when a person perceives themselves as unfairly placed in the power dynamic. This is often coupled with feelings of bitterness, contempt or disgust. For example, when an employee thinks they would be a better boss than their manager who is attempting to communicate.

Assertive Communication Style

THE FINAL VERBAL COMMUNICATION style is the Assertive Communication Style. This style of communication is rooted in confidence and self-assuredness. People who communicate in this way have confident body language and maintain eye contact; they are relaxed but engaged. They are emphatic but maintain a normal volume and tone of voice. They are secure in their stance both literally and figuratively and are willing to take the risk of rejection or a disagreeing party for the reward of collaboration. They communicate their points with a calm but firm demeanor.

In a toolbox this would be a multi-purpose tool. It's a great go-to for MOST situations.

This type of communicator is the easiest to communicate with as they are able to remain level-headed in disagreement and are not forceful in any way. They are not trying to enforce an attitude of superiority, nor are they trying to remain hidden. People respect the fact that this communicator is able to share their perspective in a concise and direct manner without being aggressive.

As you can see, there are many moving parts involved in communication. We often mix styles until we find what works, then use that style even in situations that may not work. By studying different styles of communication and becoming aware of our own motivations for using each, we can decide which to use to meet our goals. To become a more effective communicator, you'll have to stop studying and start practicing. Fail hard and be open to feedback or stick with what you're doing and suffer.

In conversation, we can understand a little more about someone else's motives or intent. The aggressive communicator is no longer "being mean to you for some reason" but is afraid of being ignored or disrespected. Rather than the passive communicator being pitiful and annoying, they are afraid and trying to protect themselves. The passive aggressive communicator perceived themselves as powerless and is trying to be heard but still socially accepted. They are no longer just mean spirited or out to get you.

When you understand the why behind a person's actions, you are better able to give the responsibility back to them. It may not be their fault they communicate in that way but it is their responsibility (not yours) to communicate in a way that meets their goals. The same is true for you. You are responsible for your communication style not theirs. The way you communicate may not be your fault, but developing your own communication skills is your responsibility. No one can do it for you and trust me you wouldn't want that anyway.

The Difference Between Being "Nice" and Being "Kind"

OUR DISCUSSION OF COMMUNICATION styles requires us to make the distinction between being "nice" and being "kind." While these two terms may seem to be describing the same thing, they are actually quite different.

The dictionary (Merriam-Webster) defines Nice (adj): "polite, pleasing, agreeable or socially acceptable." Being nice is usually what people who use a passive communication style are trying to accomplish. They believe that they must lose, and the other person must win, and that this is being nice. While it is easy to see where these people get this idea, it is ineffective as a communication style and does not serve the person in the long run. These people are generally afraid of conflict and do not want to "ruffle any feathers." Being nice while communicating looks like the following;

ASSERTIVE & KIND

- Letting the other person speak to you in any way they want

- Not sharing your perspective in fear of offending someone

- Remaining quiet when you have something valuable to say

- Taking a backseat in discussions

- Avoiding decision making and agreeing with others decisions

- Avoiding conflict at all costs

There is a much more effective way to communicate with people that doesn't require you to be aggressive or rude. Merriam-Webster defines Kind (adj): "of a sympathetic or helpful nature." When using an assertive communication style, you can be kind, that is to say 'helpful' without being passive and letting other people take advantage of you. Sometimes the most helpful thing you can do for a person is to provide more information (or politely disagree) by sharing your perspective. This is what we want to accomplish with the assertive communication style.

Being kind while communicating looks like the following;

- Hearing and listening to the other person (sympathetic)

- Allowing them to share their perspective (sympathetic)

- Sharing yours in response (helpful)

- Not being passive or aggressive, or passive-aggressive, but being direct and clear. (other communication styles are not sympathetic or helpful)

Let's run through a simple scenario that shows the difference between nice and kind.

The Situation: A coworker has crumbs on their shirt from lunch. They would be easily brushed off if the person knew they were there.

The passive "nice" person doesn't say anything. They think, "I don't want to embarrass my coworker. They might get angry and tell me to mind my own business. It's not my place to say anything." So the passive communicator says nothing, and probably averts their eyes.

The coworker walks by completely unaware of the crumbs still clinging to his shirt.

He walks by the passive aggressive communicator next who says "how professional," and the person with crumbs initially thinks, was that a compliment? Why'd they say it like that?

And the coworker walks by confused but still completely unaware of the crumbs!

The aggressive communicator simply cannot allow this unprofessionalism and loudly announces, "check out this guy with the crumbs on his shirt!"

You catch a glimpse of the coworker, completely embarrassed wiping crumbs off his shirt. He thinks, "oh I get the professional comment now. What a jerk!" Then he thinks, "that must've been why the other person looked away like that. Why didn't they tell me? I'm so embarrassed."

Now imagine that same situation except this time the passive communicator chose to be kind (remember: sympathetic and/or helpful) using assertive communication. The above scenario could've gone something like this instead:

A coworker has crumbs on their shirt from lunch. They walk by a previously passive communicator who chooses kindness. This reformed communicator approaches the coworker and uses direct speech but discreet volume to say, "there are crumbs on your shirt. I have gone an entire day without noticing strings on my pants before. I remember wishing someone had just said something to me about it."

The person might say, "shoot, thanks" or maybe laugh it off with, "I'm saving it for later." Even if they have a negative reaction, they will wipe off the crumbs and avoid embarrassment. Kindness is unaffected by how it's received.

Now that you can see the clear distinction between being nice and kind, I hope you will choose kindness over niceness in your future communications.

Recap and Action Items

In this chapter, we learned about the different communication styles and some of the benefits that come with using them. We also learned about the drawbacks to these communication styles and how they compare to assertive communication. Finally, we looked at the difference between being nice and being kind.

I challenge you to reflect on when you may have been "nice" instead of "kind" and to think of some example situations where being kind would have served you much better.

In the next chapter, we will do even more self-reflecting when we learn about self-awareness and complete a self-evaluation.

Chapter 4: Assertive Communication Skills

In this chapter, we will discuss several ways that you can self-evaluate. First, though, we are going to look at the importance of self-awareness and why you should spend time practicing and developing self-awareness in the first place.

What is Self-Awareness?

To put it simply, self-awareness is knowing yourself and how you move in the world. It is an ongoing process to develop clarity internally and externally by monitoring thoughts, emotions, behaviors and how you are perceived by others (through feedback). In order to effectively do this we want to objectively monitor patterns within ourselves and accept feedback on how we interact in the world.

Self-awareness is NOT:

- Why does everyone take advantage of me? Probably because I'm just too nice. That is why animals are better than people.

- I have too much self-awareness. Why am I so awkward - no one wants to talk to me? I don't want to talk to them either. That's just who I am.

- Why are my parents so crappy? I could've been successful.

- Why are my friends holding me back? They are so lazy.

Although many of the people in these examples are introspective, they lack self-awareness because of a common problem. Rather than exploring their internal patterns, the person focuses on finding someone or something to blame. The problem with blame is that there are circumstances that are not your fault AND still your responsibility. Let's say you get hit by another car on the way to work. If the other driver is at fault, you still have responsibilities. You still have bills and possibly a family to support with a job that you now can't drive to. Did you have a meeting right away that morning? You're probably going to be late. The accident wasn't your fault but the other driver certainly isn't going to call your boss, reschedule your meeting, or take care of your family. That is your responsibility.

The real problem with blame is that it doesn't decrease your chances of the situation repeating itself. With the car accident, rather than asking "why me" or "who is to blame", better questions to start with ask "what" or "how" rather than judgemental "why". "What was preventable?" "How can I avoid getting into future car accidents?" "What do I need to do to take care of myself right now (physically and possibly emotionally)?" etc When you become aware of your patterns, you have the power to influence outcomes. When you blame external factors (or people) for situations in your life, you give them power over your outcomes.

Now that we know what's wrong with the examples, let's practice self-awareness:

- Instead of "Why does everyone take advantage of me?" Try: What situations do I feel frustrated and think I'm being taken advantage of? What do they have in common? What situations am I most comfortable in? What do they have in common? *Prediction* This person often finds the commonality is that they say 'yes' when they mean 'no'. This is something they can change. They may feel comfortable with animals because verbal communication is not required for connection. They can reduce their chances of being taken advantage of and feel more connected with others by improving their communication skills!

- Instead of "Why am I so awkward?" Try: In what situations do I feel embarrassed and think I'm awkward? What do these situations have in common? In what situations do I think people don't want to talk to me? What resources do I have to help me? ***Prediction*** This person often finds the common thread is their lack of skill with interpersonal communication. Many people experience social anxiety, and there are just as many resources to assist.

- Instead of "Why are my parents so crappy?" Try: In what situations do I feel sad or disappointed and think I lack support? What do these situations have in common? What can I do for myself to build success? How can I support myself or build a team to support each other? ***Prediction*** This person often finds the common thread is not receiving expected outcomes. If this person listens to feedback from others, they may see a pattern of entitlement. It's also possible that their basic needs weren't met as a child. Addressing this in therapy would improve their ability to manage their feelings of disappointment, perceive failures as opportunities, and ensure their needs are met.

- Instead of "Why are my friends holding me back?" Try: What are the situations that I think my friends are holding me back? What do they have in common? What can I change? ***Prediction*** This person often finds they choose friends who match what they think about or have been told about themselves. Maybe they choose to read self-help about this topic and focus on improving themselves rather than blaming others. Maybe, they go to therapy or find a support group that helps them develop beyond these friendships.

Just like blaming others won't help us change our situation, blaming ourselves won't either. Psychologists have discovered shame is the least effective method of motivation for long term change. Remember, non-judgemental observation of our behaviors is the key to internal self-awareness. If we identify a thought or behavior pattern as helpful we do it more. Conversely if we identify it as unhelpful, we can police these thoughts appropriately or ask for help from a support group or therapist. (Have I mentioned therapy?)

Now let's practice using self-awareness to identify our communication style preference.

Self-Evaluation: Determine your Current Communication Style

Practicing self-awareness, we begin to monitor our communication patterns and ask trusted but honest people for feedback on how we are perceived. This helps us analyze our interactions and see patterns in the way others respond. Often, we exhibit a combination of all four communication styles but we can usually pin ourselves down to one style the majority of the time. Understanding this will help us communicate our own thoughts and ideas more effectively and avoid misunderstanding others' thoughts and ideas.

To examine your own communication style, start with your body language, tone of voice, and choice of words. It is also important to notice how all of these are working together as a whole. By doing this, you will be able to determine your own communication style and then decide whether it is effective or if you want to strengthen another.

Look back on the four communication styles outlined in Chapter 3. Which of these styles resonates with you most? Be honest with yourself, even if your go-to style is not the one you think is best. Spend some time reflecting on this alone.

Self-Evaluation: How Assertive are You?

In this section, you will be able to determine how assertive you are compared to your goals. First, we will talk about the different levels of assertiveness.

- Highly Assertive

If you are highly assertive, this means that you are able to express yourself appropriately in almost every situation. During interpersonal communication, all parties are able to express their needs, are satisfied with the resolution and no one believes they were overlooked or coerced. Chances are if you are reading this book, this is your goal rather than your current situation.

- Aggressive

If you are aggressive, you get what you want, or else! You don't want to waste time by asking about the needs and the feelings of others, they might ignore yours.

- Passive-Aggressive

Many people think they are being assertive but they are really being passive aggressive. If you are passive-aggressive, this usually means that you think you should have more power over your life (and probably a higher position) than you do. This is frustrating, but you're not about to express your anger publicly. You have more self-control than that. So instead you make what you think are witty comments, indirectly at-

ASSERTIVE & KIND

tacking the person. If they get mad, it's easy to say "that's not what I meant" or "I never said that" because you never did say that ... directly. You will probably suggest a rumor about the person later. Everyone does it. Rest assured, if someone is direct and challenges your communication style, you will explode in anger and aggressively communicate. Evidently that's the only way to get what you want around here.

- Passive — *When ill, fearful of conflict or uncertain*

If you are passive, you think you are ignored and others take advantage of you. You think you are nice; others see you as nice and agreeable. You are getting overwhelmed and feeling resentful because your needs aren't being met (or expressed). Most of the time you don't even know what your needs are, let alone how to ask for them. You apologize for everything and are afraid of rejection. When you try to communicate assertively, you are unable to clearly express yourself. Interpersonal communication usually ends in confusion and awkwardness.

- Assertive — *generally.*

Being assertive is the middle point between aggressiveness and passiveness, and it is said to be the happy medium. There are four characteristics associated with being an assertive person. They are as follows;

- Expressing your perspective and welcoming further communication even if people are offended

- Expressing your desires and needs

- Approaching situations and interactions in a confident manner

- Communicating effectively

WHAT IS EMPATHY?

Empathy is very important when discussing the steps that you should take to reach satisfaction when problem-solving. Empathy is quite necessary when it comes to problem solving and conflict, as it enables you to see another person's perspective. Even if you disagree, with empathy, you are able to reach a solution with compassion instead of reacting with anger. We will start by looking at the different types of empathy.

- Empathic Concern

This is the most common form of empathy. This is the type we are talking about most often when we use the term "empathy." Empathy is the ability to understand someone else's feelings, feel compassion for them and take action to help. Once you understand their feelings, it is easier to respond appropriately.

- Emotional Empathy

This type of empathy is called emotional empathy. It is what often drives compassion and the desire to help others. When someone we love starts crying, we react. Some people react by trying to cheer the person up, some react by crying along with them, and others feel compassion. The danger of emotional empathy is getting swept up in the other person's emotions and being unable to respond appropriately.

- Cognitive Empathy

The final type of empathy is cognitive empathy. This type of empathy is when you put yourself in someone else's shoes (figuratively); trying to see their perspective and understand their experience. This is a purely logical understanding of a person's emotional state.

Empathy vs. Sympathy

As I mentioned, the most common form of empathy, compassionate empathy (hereafter, empathy), is the ability to understand the feelings of another. The difference between empathy and sympathy is that sympathy only involves feeling sorry for someone else. In contrast, empathy involves putting yourself in their shoes in order to understand what they must be feeling and thinking.

Empathy is important in communicating effectively and problem-solving using assertive communication. One person is able to understand the needs of the other and express genuine interest. For this reason, problem-solving is most effective when using an assertive communication style. Each person can understand and connect with the needs of the other and meet everyone's needs to the best of their abilities.

If you pity someone or feel sympathy for them you are simply reacting to their inability to meet their needs. Often pity lacks connection and one person thinks they have it better than the other. Empathy requires humility and understanding which breeds connection and growth.

The Benefits of Empathy

Empathy can have powerful effects on relationships and life in a general sense. Empathy has the power to do all of the following and more,

- Empathy helps people manage difficult experiences.

Empathy has the power to heal. This is because we are social creatures that thrive on connection. Being present for people in their most difficult experiences requires empathy. When we have empathy, we are able to understand what others are going through, what they may need, and what we can do for them.

Empathy also bridges gaps through creating understanding. When disagreement escalates beyond conflict, reconciliation may be required. Empathy bridges the gap between the parties so reconciliation can occur.

- Empathy will strengthen your relationships.

Empathy also strengthens relationships. Empathy allows relationships to grow and promotes intimacy among people, even if only in a platonic way. Empathy creates mutual connection and understanding. When you can understand another person, this strengthens your bond.

If you have a friend that you are close with, think of how you would feel if they came to you crying. How would you feel if they told you that they were going through something tough? You would likely understand and feel compassion for them, even if you were not going through it yourself. This is empathy at work. This is why you feel so close to this person.

- Empathy will allow you to rest your mind.

Empathy can also calm your mind. This is because it allows a person to practice gratitude and brings them into the present moment. Empathy and meditation are closely linked. Meditation brings about feelings of calm and awareness, while empathy does quite the same. Practicing compassion through a loving kindness meditation can improve empathy.

- Empathy can improve your life overall.

Finally, empathy can break the silence. This means that it can lead to intimacy and connection, which also leads to dialogue among people. This can be helpful for people who have a hard time opening up and who don't readily speak their feelings or share their thoughts. It is very difficult to be open and vulnerable, especially when shame is present. If you share your experience with someone that you know will understand and not judge you, shame doesn't stand a chance.

What is Active Listening?

This section will continue our exploration of communication styles by discussing a facet of communication that is often forgotten- listening! Listening is an essential part of communication that many people forget.

Listening is just as much a part of communication as speaking. One of the keys to successful communication in relationships is being able to listen well. Listening well is a skill that must be practiced and maintained, so in this section, I will teach you how to improve your listening skills.

Listening includes what we observe with our eyes just as much as what we hear. Now that you understand both verbal and nonverbal communication (Chapter 3), we are going to look deeper into both of these to understand how to be the best communicator possible.

The first thing that makes a good listener is being able to actively listen. Active listening uses empathy and awareness, which improves your ability to be an effective assertive communicator.

Active listening involves not just hearing what is being said to you but also understanding. It involves a deeper concentration than just hearing. It involves understanding the context as a whole rather than just the words themselves. We will often hear the person speaking to us, but not really be paying attention to what they are saying. Paying close attention helps us understand the information being shared with us and then respond thoughtfully. This type of listening will help you get the most out of your conversations and interactions. Active listening smooths your transition to assertive communication.

The second thing to note when becoming a better listener is your intention. Many times, we will listen with the intent to respond. We are listening for the end of their turn so that we can say what we want to say. We may even construct what we want to say next the entire time the other person is speaking. Instead, we want to listen with the intent to understand. Listening requires an open mind. If our mind is full of thoughts about how we will respond and what we will say next, we cannot really listen and process what we are hearing.

The Benefits of Active Listening

Suppose we can actively listen with the intent to understand rather than respond. We can develop a greater understanding of other people and contribute significantly rather than superficially to the conversation. This is an important part of assertive communication because understanding the other person's needs and feelings helps us to adjust our approach accordingly. We will be better able to contribute to their well-being and have them contribute to ours.

We often think we are listening but there is a big difference between hearing and listening. You may hear the individual words that a person is saying, but not understand what they are trying to say. By not listening, it's easy to forget what the person was talking about just a few short minutes after the conversation.

When using the other styles of communication, most of the focus is on the self. A person using passive, aggressive, or passive-aggressive communication is usually concerned with how they appear, how others will react to them, and how to get what they want. Because of this, they are likely only *hearing* the other person rather than listening to understand.

In assertive communication, listening is very important. Assertive communicators are concerned with the well-being of those they interact with and play a part in improving their well-being, if possible. They place importance on listening and understanding the other person in order to collaborate and create mutually beneficial outcomes.

How to Use Empathetic Dialogue

It is important to avoid communication styles that include judging, blaming, shaming, etc yourself or others. As long as you remember this, you will be closer to expressing yourself in an assertive way.

An example of effective, empathetic, assertive communication is the following;

"I heard you talking on the phone at 3am. I felt frustrated when I woke up to the sound of you talking because I need sleep. Please talk on the phone before midnight."

In this example, the person recognizes their feelings and associated needs. From there, they have verbalized this need and are expressing it to the person who is involved in the situation without blame. You can also end with an invitation to collaborate on a solution. Be careful not to say "you made me frustrated when you woke me up". No one can make you feel an emotion. You were frustrated because you needed sleep. If you didn't need sleep you may not have been frustrated.

This kind of assertive communication aims to resolve a situation to the satisfaction of all parties. It aims to promote understanding and compassion instead of judgement or dismissal as in passive and aggressive communication styles. Assertive communication diffuses situations before they escalate. When both parties express themselves through assertive communication, situations are resolved well before anger has built up to the point of an outburst.

Conflict is not an inherently negative or violent thing. It does not have to lead to the breakdown of relationships, yelling or screaming. It does not have to involve a dominant party and a submissive party or an expresser and a listener. Conflict can be seen in a positive way and promote sharing educated opinions and individual perspectives. This is how situations and relationships can be improved rather than harmed. By allowing yourself to clearly and calmly express your thoughts and feelings, you are practicing self-respect (and avoiding unintentionally building anger or resentment).

When using assertive communication, you must examine your thoughts, feelings and values. In this way, every person is accountable for what they are actually feeling. Often people cover up vulnerable emotions with anger and aggression. When you use assertive communication, you get used to expressing your feelings clearly and effectively. In conflict resolution everyone is aware of what is needed and how to fulfill that need. Sometimes, when there is conflict, you must try to discern what the other person needs or wants in order to resolve the conflict. With passive communicators it can be difficult because only the person themselves knows what they need. If they express it to you in simple and clear terms, you can instead skip right to the point of resolution. If you have to spend the time trying to figure out what it is they need, conflicts can get blown out of proportion or build feelings of resentment. For this reason, using assertive communication helps people to express and meet their needs.

Recap and Action Items

In this chapter, you took stock of your own communication style and your level of assertiveness. Now that you know both of these reflect on how you would like to change. For example, you want to become more assertive and stop using a passive communication style.

We also discussed empathy and how to use empathetic communication. This will take practice, but try to spend some time over the next several days getting in touch with the empathetic part of yourself. You could do this as you are walking down the street and you see a homeless individual, or when you are at home, and your kids are struggling with their homework. Try to practice empathy and empathetic communication.

Chapter 5: Setting Boundaries

Empathy without boundaries leaves both people helpless to tidal waves of emotion. Relationships that have healthy boundaries are more secure compared to the ones that don't. Creating boundaries together means that both people will better understand what type of relationship they have together. The problem is, a person must be comfortable with assertive communication in order to set healthy boundaries. In this chapter, we will learn how to set boundaries and why this is so important.

What are Boundaries?

Boundaries are a way for you to express the things that make you comfortable or uncomfortable, or what you would like to happen or not happen within your relationship. Setting and maintaining boundaries is an important part of being assertive in your relationship and taking care of yourself within that relationship.

Boundaries are not only present in romantic relationships. For instance, here is the definition of a professional relationship; "A professional relationship is an ongoing interaction between two individuals who follow established boundaries that are deemed appropriate under their governing standards." Boundaries exist in all relationships.

The Importance of Setting Boundaries

Boundaries are important because they show people what you will and will not accept. This shows people that you respect yourself and that you value your needs. To put it simply, this demonstrates your level of self-respect.

A person with a healthy level of self-respect is able to identify when their needs are not being met or are not being prioritized. If they can recognize this, they are respecting themselves enough to assertively let the other person know. On the other hand, a person who does not respect themselves does not have the ability to recognize what their needs are, let alone if they are being met. This makes it impossible to let the other person know if things need to change. People who suffer from low self-respect will often take responsibility for both sides of the relationship. They personalize disagreements and think they are not doing enough or not doing things right, and that is why the other person is unhappy. The person often ignores their own needs in favor of "making" the other person happy. There aren't enough times where this person stops to think, "What are my needs?" or "Are my needs being met?". If a person ignores their needs long enough a few things happen. They become unaware of their needs, they build up resentment, feel guilty about feeling resentful, and have no idea why any of these things are happening.

- Being assertive improves your ability to be open, secure, and honest in relationships. It also helps you identify when the relationship you are in is unhealthy.

The concept is simple, really - if you have a healthy level of self-respect, you are able to recognize your own wants and needs and express them appropriately. If you have low self-respect, you are unable to recognize your wants and needs. Basically, you don't respect yourself enough to express your needs. An unhealthy relationship is described as, "a relationship where one or more of the people involved exhibit behaviors that are not healthy and are not founded in mutual respect." Your relationship cannot be healthy if you don't respect yourself.

Having healthy self-respect will reduce your likelihood of anxiety, abandonment issues, and habits of avoidance. You will express and fulfill your own needs, regardless of the other person's actions. You will be comfortable expressing your genuine feelings and listening to others' feelings as well. You will not take things personally because you understand the other person (using your advanced empathic abilities), and know that ultimately their feelings are their responsibility. This is why those who respect themselves, speak assertively despite fear of the other person's reaction. Allowing others to have power over their own feelings is the greatest gift you can give.

HOW TO SET BOUNDARIES

To set boundaries, there are a few things that you must remember.

1. Speak Up

When a relationship is healthy, the people in the relationship are comfortable with talking about a problem rather than holding it in. Each person can get what they need from the relationship. Honest, open, and clear communication is crucial when it comes to having a healthy relationship. The first step into building one is to make sure both people understand each other's needs and expectations.

1. Respect

Being assertive involves respecting yourself and the other person and letting them know when you are not feeling respected.

1. Be Consistent

Your actions dictate your boundaries even more than your words. If you say no, but do it anyway, you are really saying yes. Most people naturally resist change, even if it is positive. If you've been saying yes to every-

ASSERTIVE & KIND

thing, others have developed a habit of hearing yes from you. This can be difficult and confusing for them (and you)..

Healthy boundaries in romantic relationships should not restrict the following;

- Participating in hobbies and activities that you enjoy without your partner.

- Going out with friends or other people without your partner.

- Not needing to share passwords to your social media, phone, or email.

- Respecting each other's individual needs and preferences.

Healthy boundaries in work relationships should not restrict the following;

- Separating personal life from work life

- Addressing concerns clearly and respectfully

- Taking an appropriate amount of time off

- Discussing individual/company needs & how they are sometimes at odds

- Saying no to unethical behavior

- Addressing unhelpful or unhealthy behaviors

Figuring Out Your Feelings

Being aware of your thoughts and emotions is important in being able to use assertive communication to set boundaries. For many people, this is a challenge. We live in a world where it's easier to distract yourself than look inward. This is due to how much easier and more enjoyable it is to distract yourself in the moment. We are also being sold as a means of distraction everywhere we go. Looking inward and getting in touch with your feelings will take practice, but it will become easier the more you do it. Here's how:

- Commit

The first step to listening to your feelings is committing to doing so. Commitment requires consistency. If you are not committed, it will prove difficult for you to really examine yourself when it's easier to do anything else in the moment. Once you begin listening to your feelings, you will be able to accept them as they are and possibly take action toward improving your situation. The first step to doing this is noticing what those emotions are.

- Notice Sensations In Your Body

Once you have committed to looking deep within yourself, the best place to start is to notice when something within you feels different. When we feel emotions, we often feel them manifested somewhere in our bodies. A tightness in your chest or a sinking feeling in your stomach, is usually an indication that you are experiencing some type of emotion. Even if you are not sure what the emotion is, noticing the signs within your body that signal when you are feeling an emotion is a great first step. Many people will feel an emotion and ignore it by distracting themselves, project it on another person and lash out at them, or anything in between. Distraction keeps people from looking inward to really explore the feeling or what thoughts, beliefs and situations brought it up for them. Take a second now to notice how your body

ASSERTIVE & KIND

feels. Scan your body for tightness or feelings of unrest. You may be feeling some emotions right now. Pay attention to the changes that happen within your body when you experience an emotion so that the next time you feel it, you notice it instead of pushing it away.

- Give The Feelings A Name

After noticing where you are feeling emotions in your body, focus on that area and then give the emotion a name. We are all aware of emotions like fear, anger, happiness, surprise, and sadness. These emotions are a good place to begin. Resources like an emotion wheel can be helpful if you get stuck.

- Go Deeper

As we become adults, our emotions become more complex than just the five listed above. We are able to experience deeper and more complicated emotions such as shame, anxiety, desperation, shock, doubt, ambiguity, and so on. Once you are comfortable noticing and naming your emotions in a simple way, try to look at them a little deeper and figure out if the emotion you thought was sadness is actually more disappointment, for example. Suppose you are unsure of what some of these more complex emotions may be. In that case, you can name the emotion in the simpler sense (sadness, for example) and then take this word to a thesaurus or an emotion chart online in order to see what other emotions this could be related to that could better describe exactly what you are feeling.

Giving yourself a broader vocabulary of emotions will help you to express yourself in more depth. You can develop a deeper understanding of yourself and others can develop a deeper understanding of you as well. Naming the emotions you feel when you notice them will allow you to express these emotions to other people in assertive communication when the time comes.

Speak Using "I" Statements

Once you take all of these steps, you can begin to speak using "I" statements. An "I" statement is how you express your needs in the form of boundaries. In the following section, we will look at some examples of boundaries using "I" statements.

"I" statements allow us to speak assertively and disagree with the other person without blaming, shaming and judging. Unfortunately, it is quite common to hear someone express their emotions like this, "you make me feel ..."

This phrase shows a lack of ownership of our own emotions, as if other people have control over us. This might be difficult to hear at first but it will give you incredible power:

Your thoughts and beliefs influence your emotions, then you act or react.

Still don't believe me? Let's walk through a hypothetical example:

You wave to 10 strangers. A few people are happy, some are uncomfortable, many are annoyed, one is jealous. Your action was the same but the feelings and outcomes were different. Why? Because they are different people, with different thoughts and experiences and belief systems. The people who felt happy might have thought it's nice to see such a polite person. The people who felt uncomfortable might have wondered why you were waving, or if you were making fun of them. Those who felt annoyed might have thought, "why are you just waving to people? Don't you have anything better to do?" The person who felt jealous might have thought, "I wish I wasn't so afraid of waving to people, why can't I be friendly like that." This means another person's actions are not the direct cause of *your* emotions, otherwise everyone's reaction would've been the same.

The opposite of an "I" statement is a "you" statement as in: "you MAKE me feel."

Why do so many people even use this phrase and allow others to control their emotions and in turn actions? It's because we want to find the source of the problem and fix it. BUT we want to be part of the problem. We want to protect ourselves from guilt or shame. So when we try to communicate our feelings we place blame rather than take ownership. The feelings statement comes out as, "you make me feel ..." This is called a "you" statement. This is a blaming statement and usually elicits a defensive response.

The opposite (and a more accurate way to state your feelings) is an "I" statement. I statements usually have 4 pieces:

I feel ____

when ____

because ____

I need ____.

"I feel" is usually how the feeling statement begins. We've already spent a significant part of the last few chapters on expressing feelings so that part should be clear. Feel free to reread if you're stuck.

"When" is describing the situation, again, try to focus on your experience of the situation rather than blame. Remember it's your perception of the situation that sparks the emotion.

"Because" is usually where you share your values, thoughts etc. Keep in mind everyone may not share your values and the world is a better place because people's values are different, not despite this fact.

"I need" is the assertive statement that sets a boundary. There's no need for disrespect or an aggressive tone. Demands and ultimatums don't belong here either. Firm, clear statements of what you need and release the outcome.

Let Go of the Outcome

An important but very difficult part of using "I" statements and setting boundaries is letting go of your expectations. The perfect "I" statement delivered assertively in the right setting with a loved one may still be met with resistance or push back. People naturally resist change. The first few times they push back, don't personalize it and assume they love you or care about you or respect you. Maybe they are human beings struggling as well. Notice how I said *the first few times*. Address this with the other person. "I feel upset when others shout at me. I need loving support and connection."

Every interaction is a datapoint that creates a picture of your relationship with a person. With consistency you'll be able to separate those who respect your boundaries, those just who need a few reminders of your boundaries, and those who are not able to respect them. From there you can build space or connection as needed. Don't get caught up in your desire to be in a relationship that you aren't paying attention to whether or not you actually like talking to the person. Also, don't focus so much on getting a compassionate response that you see anything less as a communication failure.

Examples of Building Boundaries Using "I Statements"

"I value sleep, please don't call me after 10pm. My phone will be on silent after 10pm."

"I am tired. I need more sleep. Please take a turn waking up with the baby. Let's wake up every other night."

"I am not comfortable talking about our sex life in public. Please don't discuss things like that when we are spending time with friends. Let's talk about this at home where we have privacy."

"I feel upset when I'm spoken to like that. Please use a different tone of voice. Let's take a break and regroup in 15 min."

While writing this example my 10 year old daughter laughed at me saying, "if I told the boys at school that when they were being rude they'd stop listening to me at "I feel". They don't care how I feel." It was a good reminder that there are practical situations, where it's better to start by getting to the point. While skipping the feeling piece prevents a deeper connection, stating your request respectfully keeps the connection from being severed completely.

If a person you are not close to is using a tone with you, it's ok to not share the feeling piece. "Please use a different tone of voice. If not, I can come back in 15 min." You don't have to give a speech about respect or match their tone. Keep it simple and prioritize managing your emotions.

"I enjoy spending quality time with you. Please make time to spend with me without being distracted. Let's set a time."

Recap and Action Items

Now that you understand boundaries and the use of "I" statements, try to come up with some boundaries that you wish to set with the people in your life. This can be with your significant other, family members, or friends. Boundaries can also be set in real-time when a person you are interacting with does or says something that you are not okay with. Write down some of your boundaries in the form of "I" statements and voice them to the people in your life. Start small with people that you trust and talk to them about what you're trying to do!

Chapter 6: Communicating In An Emotional State

In this chapter, we will explore what happens when you communicate in an emotionally-charged state. Some of the techniques you can use to calm your mind (and body) before engaging in confrontation or a challenging, emotional conversation.

Why you Should Not Communicate When in an Emotionally Charged State

When people do not calm down before speaking or addressing the situation, they will generally choose one of two options. They will either avoid the situation with passive communication or enter the situation defensively with an aggressive communication style. Neither of these methods is effective, and I will show you several benefits of addressing the situation after calming your mind and body in order to speak assertively.

The Benefits of Calming Down Before Speaking

- **You are able to Really Listen to the Other Person.**

There is a big difference between hearing and listening. You may hear the individual words that a person is saying, but this is not the same as understanding what they are saying to you.

When you speak out in an emotionally charged state, you are unable to listen to the other person. You may hear them, but you do not listen with the intent to understand because you are focused on your emotions and what you want to say next.

- **People will React to you Differently.**

I touched on this earlier in the book, but it is so important that we will revisit it again here. When you approach a conversation in an emotionally-charged state (for example, using aggressive communication), other people will shut down or fight back in response. They do this because they feel threatened. This style of communication leaves no room for discussion or resolution.

Emotions are contagious. Studies suggest that this comes from a survival instinct. If you saw someone was afraid, it's probably something for you to fear as well. It's not a perfect system; it's primitive survival instincts. These instincts are in place for the times when immediate action is required in order to stay alive. If we know this, we can manage our own emotional state and stop the spread of fear.

Instead, suppose you calm down and approach the situation in an assertive and calm manner. In that case, the chances of the other people responding in kind are greatly increased. I'm not saying that by showing emotional vulnerability, you will always receive genuine concern for you and what you have to say. However, it's more likely to create a constructive and positive interaction instead of a negative one.

- **It Gives you Time to Think and Process Before Reacting.**

If you are emotionally charged and take time to calm yourself before reacting emotionally, this gives you time to reflect and think about the situation. This may lead you to see it more clearly or see a new perspective that you could not see before. This can serve you in finding a creative solution or deciding how to respond. Sometimes, all it takes is a few deep breaths, and sometimes you need to sleep on it. Either way, as long as you give yourself the time and space you need, you will be better off.

Strategies for Calming Yourself Before Speaking

To close this chapter, I will present several emotion regulation techniques that will help you in those times where you are feeling sad, hurt, angry, embarrassed or a combination of all of these emotions. Whether you are a person who tends to act on your feelings with aggression and verbal outbursts, or you are a person who reacts by shutting down, making comments under your breath and avoiding the situation as a whole, these techniques will prove quite useful in your journey of finding effective emotion regulation. This way, you can revisit the situation or conversation when you are feeling more level-headed.

1. Count to Ten

When you feel the anger inside you instead of shutting it down or allowing it to make your blood boil, count up to ten (or fifty depending on your level of anger or emotion). If you are furious or emotional, make it 100. This technique helps give you time to calm yourself physically. Your heart rate will slow down to a normal level, and your adrenaline responses will subside as well. This allows you to take a step back and think more clearly.

1. Take Deep Breaths

When you are afraid, angry or experiencing intense emotion, your breathing becomes shallow and short. Focus on your breath by slowing it down and focus on inhaling deep and exhaling long breaths. Inhale through your nose and exhale through your mouth. Focusing on your breathing helps you calm yourself and gives your brain the oxygen it needs to think clearly.

1. Repeat a Mantra

Having a mantra may seem a little unconventional, but it can be quite helpful in times of intense emotion. A mantra is a word or a phrase that you repeat which is designed to help you concentrate on meditation. In day-to-day life, though, it helps bring your consciousness back to the moment, just like meditation does. Your mantra can be anything, such as "relax," "I'm in control of my emotions," or anything that helps you to calm yourself at the moment. Decide on your mantra in a moment of calm and quiet so that it is there in the back of your mind when you need it in a moment of intense emotion.

1. Stretch Your Body

Stretching is a good practice for moments of intense emotion because it helps to bring you back down to earth. It reconnects you with your body and your muscles, which will help bring you to the moment and will help with your blood flow. Any stretches are good; neck rolls, leg stretches, or shoulder rolls are great.

1. Use Visualization

This is a great tool for when it is difficult to control your emotional state. When a person is visualizing, the person is actively aware that the things they're visualizing are not real but are flexing their creative muscles. The interesting part is that our minds can't identify the difference between what we are imagining and what we are doing. In other words, your mind isn't able to distinguish the difference between real life, an imagined future, or a memory. Rather, the mind is under the impression that everything we see is real. This is proven by numerous brain scans that scientists have conducted over the years, where they discovered that the brain shows little distinction in activity when someone is observing something in the real world compared to when a person is visualizing.

This is extremely important because it suggests that by using visualization, people can grease the wheels of skill development without the requirement of performing those actions physically. For example, the person can imagine their ideal relaxing scenario without having to get themselves there physically.

Using the technique of imagining calming yourself, you can help effectively rewire your brain to build new patterns, habits, and behaviors. This makes completing these tasks in the real world far less difficult. For example, imagining a relaxing scenario when you feel anger coming on will eventually make it easier for your brain and body to relax without having to use visualization. Due to this, you will feel much calmer when you practice relaxation in times of anger.

To begin practicing this, go somewhere quiet and get comfortable. Close your eyes and visualize your ideal relaxing scene. Imagine you are there. Imagine the sights, smells, sounds, and feelings that you would be experiencing. By doing this, you are tricking your brain into thinking you are in this scene, which will bring you feelings of relaxation, joy, and comfort. Another practice is to visualize experiencing an intense emotion and the steps you would take to manage those emotions. Imagine yourself at the height of emotion, taking deep breaths, stretching, walking, counting and calming down on your own. This scenario is important to practice as you can't avoid intense emotions but you can manage them.

It is also important to notice that you've probably already been using visualization for self-sabotage. Many people imagine worst case scenarios and create their own future filled with fear and anxiety. Fear is probably a reason you haven't spoken assertively before reading this book. Maybe you imagined that if you were direct, the other person would yell. Maybe you imagined they would feel hurt. Your brain can't tell the difference, so you have been torturing yourself with things that may not happen. In the rare chance they do happen just as you imagine, you are forcing yourself to experience them MULTIPLE TIMES!

All I'm saying is please use visualization as a force for good rather than evil. You'll thank you later.

1. Stop What You Are Doing

If you start yelling out everything that you have wanted to say for so long but you didn't want it to come out in anger like this either, make yourself stop talking. Glue your lips together, and do not allow yourself to open them for a few minutes. This time where you cannot allow yourself to spit out a slew of words that you do not mean will give you some time to think before you decide what you want to say or do. Walk away, right it out, move your body away from the situation. Don't waste the important things you have to say in an outburst. When you finally say what you haven't been able to, be proud to deliver it in a clear and direct way.

1. Exercise

Exercise does great things for your body, especially in times of intense anger. The positive feelings of "runner's high" that you get after doing exercise will help to dispel some of your anger and/or built-up resentment. Also, directing your intense emotions to the gym will help you harness and move the emotion through your body in a healthy way.

Getting active is a great solution when you have the time. Often, when people feel intense emotion, they do not want to get up and do something physical. However, exercising is a great way to relieve stress and move pent up emotion. You don't have to spend hours at the gym to reap the benefits; you can simply do light exercise. One way to do this is to go for a quick walk to allow your brain to release the endorphins that make you feel good. People get the most benefit from exercise if they do it for at least 30 minutes per day. Small exercise activities will add up over the course of a day. Here are some suggestions that you can try to incorporate into your schedule:

- Play an active game with your family/friends (e.g., ping pong, Wii)

- Find an exercise partner and hold each other accountable

- Parking your car as far as you can and get yourself to walk to wherever you're going

- Walk to do your errands instead of driving

- If you have an animal, take him/her out for a walk (I'm sure your cat will love it)

- Play some music and dance around (in private if you must)

1. Write Your Feelings

There are likely many things that you want to say but that you know would do more harm than good, especially if you say them in a time of intense emotion or anger. Write these things down. This way, you are still expressing yourself and your anger, but you are not hurting anyone or your relationships by doing so. This helps you process your emotions by examining them from afar to decide the best course of action.

1. Rant

Ranting to someone who is not involved in the situation can help you express yourself without offending someone involved and risking damaging your relationship. Healthy ranting to a third party helps allow you to express yourself. After your rant, switch modes to process the situation, your thoughts, and feelings. The perspective of a person who is not involved is often very useful if you can remain open to feedback.

1. Try to Laugh

Laughing can help to diffuse your anger or feel more positive. Laughing is strong medicine, so making yourself laugh when feeling intense emotions can help you to relax a little and take a step back. Watching a funny show, talking to a friend who makes you laugh, or scrolling the internet for funny content are all ways of doing this.

More Relaxation Strategies

The most effective way of controlling anger or diffusing your emotions involves relaxation. If you feel like you are feeling resentful but your level of anger is not as much the problem as the rate at which it recurs, trying to practice relaxation techniques will prove quite useful.

A quick and easy relaxation technique is to remind yourself to relax. Simply remembering that this is the goal will help you stop and think about the techniques stored in the back of your mind, giving you time to recall them. This will not only help you relax but will distract you from your emotion long enough to slow the escalation. Then, when you remember it, you may not feel that it is as intense as you first thought.

When the emotion takes over your body, it can be difficult to think clearly or rationally. Remember you are in charge of your emotions, there are several techniques that you can try in order to ensure that you don't lash out at others when you are defensive or trying to protect yourself.

Mindfulness

Mindfulness is a type of mental training practice that involves focusing your mind on your thoughts and sensations in the present moment. This includes your current emotions, physical sensations, and passing thoughts. Mindfulness usually involves breathing practice, mental imagery, awareness of your mind and body, and muscle and body relaxation. This can be beneficial in emotion regulation as it will help you to connect to your body and mind. This connection allows you to control your emotions.

The most popular reason people decide to learn meditation is to achieve mindfulness to combat mental obstacles. If you are someone that lives a very fast-paced and stressful life, mindfulness and meditation can help you manage your own thoughts and emotions to bring you more peace. Many mental health professionals encourage the study and practice of meditation and mindfulness techniques to promote a healthier brain and mind.

To get into a state of mindfulness you must get quiet and observe, without judgment, everything that occurs within your body. Most of the time, we are mindlessly moving through the world, acting without thought. In this state we say and do things that are not moving us toward our goals. When it comes to emotion regulation, this comes in the form of acting defensively instead of using the techniques in this book. One way to avoid this is by using mindfulness.

How To Use Mindfulness To Manage Your Emotions

There are many ways that a person can practice mindfulness to manage their emotions. You could simply just sit quietly for five minutes and concentrate on the environment around you. Pay attention to the fact that you have thoughts going through your mind. Just observe then, don't grab onto any of them. Don't believe what you think, just see them as clouds passing by, or items on a conveyor belt.

When your emotions don't have thoughts to fuel them, they will do what they are supposed to: rise, fall and dissipate. If you are a beginner at mindfulness, consider taking meditation classes to get a good foundation. As a beginner, try to practice mindfulness via guided sessions. Once you get a good grip on it, you can begin to just start practicing mindfulness everywhere you go by using some of the techniques you've learned.

Sample Mindfulness Exercise

Get quiet and sit with yourself in silence. Close your eyes. You must let your thoughts drift by, noticing but not judging them. Pay attention to the sensations in your body; if there is tightness or tension anywhere, the feeling of your chest rising and falling with each breath, the weight of your body on the chair or bed you are sitting on. Notice also your emotions and feelings. By doing this over and over again, you will be able to eventually focus on your body with less and less distracting thoughts. When your thoughts start to distract you, bring your attention back to your body and your breathing. Being able to reach a state like this allows you to reconnect with your body from the inside. Instead of letting your what-if thoughts feed your anxiety ad infinitum, interrupt the cycle. Your anxiety will not escalate to the level it normally would without thoughts, judgements, and worries feeding it.

How to Use Mindfulness During Assertive Communication

By using mindfulness to focus on the body, your thoughts become things separate from you that you can manipulate and untangle, resulting in a reduction in stress level and a calm emotional state. Mindfulness and meditation are some of the many things known for bringing about a state of relaxation and calm.

During a heated conversation, our mind begins to race and we try to desperately grab at all the thoughts we can for the perfect thing to say. However, when we take time to sit in silence, breathe, and sort through everything we are thinking and feeling through a non-judgmental lens, we gain clarity. This clarification makes it much easier for your body to feel at peace, and allows your mind to be more open and receptive. This is where assertive communication lives. Once you acknowledge your thoughts and feelings without judging them, you can clearly express them in an assertive way.

Recap and Action Items

Now that you understand mindfulness and how it can be used during assertive communication, try the mindfulness exercise that I described in this chapter on your own. Be sure to do so in a quiet location, free of distractions. Notice how you feel at the start and end of the exercise. Do you feel more relaxed or calm after?

Try using this technique the next time you are met with an emotionally challenging situation. Notice what difference it makes for your conflict resolution skills.

Chapter 7: Frequently Asked Questions (FAQ)

In this chapter, you will benefit from reading the answers that I have given to the most frequently asked questions regarding the topic of assertive communication. Return to this chapter anytime you have a question or need clarification about a topic.

Question 1: What is the Difference Between Assertive Communication and Aggressive Communication?

When we approach a situation with a demand, or in an aggressive way, the other person will often shut down emotionally, and the conversation cannot reach a resolution. This is because it results in both people feeling defensive and they react to each other rather than collaborate to reach a resolution. If you use assertive communication to make a request or to address an issue, the chances of coming to a resolution are much higher. This works in your favor.

While it may seem like this will be hard to remember at the moment, it will come more naturally the more you practice it. If you forget and are unsure of how you can communicate assertively, one helpful thing that you can do is remember what type of communication you do NOT want to use.

Assertive communication takes the other person's needs into account while being direct and clear about your own needs. Some people shy away from being assertive because they think that sharing an unpopular opinion directly is aggressive. Being aggressive means demanding what you want without regard to anyone else. Many times being aggressive involves silencing others with your tone, volume, intimidating stature or simply by talking over them. Being assertive means considering another person's point of view AND being firm about what you need/want, even if the other person doesn't like it. You can be firm and direct while still treating a person with respect.

Just because someone doesn't like something doesn't make it wrong, bad, or something that should be changed. For example, I didn't like brushing my teeth as a kid but as an adult I'm glad I did it anyway.

Question 2: How Can I Stop Letting People Push Me Around?

Practice. Practice. Practice.

Learning how to be assertive is an important skill to have in life as it is commonly used and respected in adults. If you find that you are suffering from the "Yes" syndrome, you may need to work on respecting yourself enough to recognize your own needs and wants.

We discussed self-respect throughout this book and how improving it can improve your assertive communication skills. This is not something that will change overnight, but with time and self-reflection, you will begin to see improvements, and thus, your ability to assert yourself and stop letting people push you around. Start small. Be patient. Be consistent!

Question 3: How Can I Communicate Assertively in a Position of Authority?

This is a great question and one that many people struggle with! To answer this question, we must ask ourselves what we look for in a person of authority or in a leader. We can then examine how you can lead and influence when you are in a position of authority, using the right body language and assertive communication techniques.

Understanding this concept will allow you to use it to your advantage by choosing what type of messages you wish to send using your body language and your choice of communication style. As a leader, it is important to know how to say things in a way that commands attention and respect and gets people listening.

As humans, the traits we desire in a leader are somewhat universal. We want to feel like we can trust our leader. We also want to feel confident that they will speak up and advocate for us. We want to be heard and understood, especially when they are required to make decisions on our behalf that will benefit us. We want them to be the confident and self-assured face that represents us, but we also want them to be relatable.

While it may seem impossible to achieve all of these different things at once, I assure you it is possible. In this section, we will learn how to use assertive communication and assertive body language.

When it comes to choosing a leader, everyone wants someone that is confident in an area where most people are not. Where most feel fear and uncertainty, the leader feels confidence and security in their choices. They are not over-confident, however, as this makes people fear naivety. Confidence is often underestimated as a tool for leadership. Yes, the choices a leader makes on behalf of their people are important, but people want someone to believe in, and they will not believe in someone that does not appear to believe in themselves. The good news is that humans have a difficult time distinguishing real confidence from performed, false confidence. Because of this, when in a position of authority, you must learn how to appear confident and show confidence using the proper body language and communication style. Below, we will look at how to do this.

- Nonverbal Communication of a Leader

So how exactly do we show our people that we are confident? This comes down to nonverbal communication. We can say as many times as we like that we are confident in what we are saying, but if our body language does not show this, we are not convincing. We are going to examine the body language of each part of a leader's body. It helps to imagine a leader you trust or imagine someone you would want to lead by. Get a picture in your mind's eye before reading the next paragraph. For suggestions, maybe they are someone speaking in front of an office of people, maybe a captain of a sport's team, maybe a chef in a restaurant. This leader does not have to be famous or of political status; all respected leaders share very similar body language. Now that we have this image in mind, we are going to examine it from head to toe. Confident nonverbal communication looks like the following:

The number one spot we are going to discuss is the arms and hands. Because leaders often speak to large groups of people or speak to people from a distance, the arms and hands are very important. From a distance, this will be what they can see if they cannot make out the face or if they are not within earshot. A leader wants their arms and hands to demonstrate ease and comfort with what they are saying and what they stand for. If you have ever seen a leader speak in a video, but you could not hear the sound, you can tell that they are a leader even without knowing who they are. This is because of their gestures and movements. Keeping your hands out and visible is a sign that you are confident and that you have nothing to hide. As humans, we tend to feel insecure if we cannot see a person's hands, especially if they lead us. Keeping your hands out and visible for all to see shows that you are being transparent and are confident in what you are standing for. While keeping your hands out, it is important to notice what they're doing. If they are fidgeting with their hair or their clothing or something on the table in front of them, they will appear nervous or anxious. If their leader appears nervous and anxious, the people will not feel secure in their leadership skills. The arms play an important role in this as well. If the arms are moving and gesturing along with what the person is saying, they appear to be enthused and passionate about what they are saying. This makes them appear to be really believing what they are saying, whereas if they are standing with their arms stiffly at their side, or if their arms are barely moving, it makes them seem rehearsed and like they are not invested in their own words. Gestures that are in tune with the content of one's speech and that are not too aggressive or over the top are best. Too many gestures can also seem rehearsed and like the person is over trying to engage people. There is a sweet spot right in the middle that feels natural and confident.

The next section we will examine is the stance and the feet to follow the arms and hands. As mentioned earlier in chapter two, the feet are an often forgotten piece to the puzzle of body language. The feet should be firmly planted on the ground, facing forward and not shifting nervously. While you don't want to stand like a statue, you do not want to be pacing or moving them in a way that demonstrates nerves. Leaders take up space. Both with their arm gestures and their feet. The stance is created by where the feet are placed. In a confident stance, the feet are wide enough that you are taking up space. If your feet are shoulder-width apart, this is an appropriate amount of space that is proportionate to your body size. Taking up space shows that you are secure in your position, that you are not trying to make yourself small to fit in anywhere, that you are unafraid to be seen.

As with stance, posture is a demonstrator of how you feel about yourself and your position. A leader will stand with their shoulders back, their chest out and open. This is another way to take up space. Your shoulders will take up space just as your feet will, and this demonstrates confidence in yourself. Hunching your shoulders, closing up your chest space, and folding yourself down is an indicator that you are trying not to be noticed or that you are not confident. Appearing too rigid and upright can make someone seem intimidating and overly uptight, so avoid being too rigid. A nice confident but comfortable posture includes the shoulders back and the hips semi-forward.

The posture of the head is important for demonstrating confidence as well. The chin should be upright, and the head should be facing forward. The head should be fairly stable when speaking or standing and even walking, as this is a natural demonstrator of confidence. Leaders avoid lowering their head or moving it from side to side as they speak as this can make them appear frantic. A leader who appears frantic is not one that people will readily trust with their best interests.

The clothing a leader wears can vary greatly by culture and region, but the clothing choice must be of a professional nature in a general sense. Professional can look like a suit, a dress, or traditional clothing, whichever is most appropriate for the setting. The choice of clothing demonstrates respect for the environment that you are in and concern for your image. Included in this are the hair and hygiene. Someone who appears to put time and effort into their clothing, appearance, and personal maintenance will appear to be prepared to take care of matters for their cause. If someone turns up to lead and are unkempt and unclean, they will give off the impression that they cannot take care of matters because they cannot take care of themselves.

- Verbal Assertive Communication of a Leader

LEADING AND BEING PERSUASIVE is a skill that involves many components but that can have limitless positive effects on your life. As with everything else in life, leading and communicating requires a delicate balance of possessing enough of the positive qualities, like confidence and assertiveness, without being too much of them, to avoid having the negative qualities (over-confident, narcissistic). By ensuring that you remain at just the right level of confidence and assertiveness without being aggressive or narcissistic, you will be able to have people respect you.

For example, if you are someone who manages employees, you want them to put in good work for you each and every day. To achieve this result, it is important to be assertive and fair with your staff's individual members. By doing this, they will feel noticed and respected by you. When it comes time to give them feedback about their performance, try giving them feedback and praise within the same conversation. This will leave them feeling as though you care about them and notice their positive efforts and will also make them more receptive to hearing your feedback.

Recap and Action Items

As people work through the process of practicing assertive communication, there are often questions that present themselves. Think of some questions that you might have about this work or the contents of this book. Write them down and spend some time reviewing the chapters in this book or finding peer support online.

Chapter 8: Traps That You May Fall Into When Communicating Assertively

This chapter will discuss some of the most common obstacles that people face when trying to communicate assertively. If you are able to understand these obstacles, you will then be able to understand how to prevent or combat them. If you are able to combat them, you will be able to get much closer to reaching your goal of being a more assertive person.

The Most Common Traps that Catch People When Trying to Communicate Assertively

1. You Don't Know What You Want.

If you do not understand what you want, it will be difficult for you to effectively and clearly communicate your wants and needs. Assertive communication is about expressing yourself calmly and effectively. When you do not know what it is that you want, you are more likely to use passive communication.

1. You Think Your Needs Don't Matter.

Depending on the type of family you grew up in, you may have been raised to feel like you are not valued and that you don't have a voice. In this type of family dynamic, your opinions and wants were not acknowledged or taken seriously. Remember, your parents are people too, there's no handbook that comes with parenting. Your parents themselves likely did not have, and therefore could not model, good relationship skills such as; conflict resolution, healthy boundaries, cooperation, and assertiveness. They may even be abusive, controlling, preoccupied, manipulative, interfering, or inconsistent. As a result, you may have felt emotionally abandoned. Children that grow up in that environment often feel insecure, anxious, and unsafe. They end up in unhealthy relationships and situations with the uncomfortable but familiar pattern of struggling to identify and express their emotional needs. This book is not a replacement for counseling. However, it can help you break free from these patterns and grow into an assertive individual who recognizes the importance of your own needs, no matter what age you are now.

1. You Want To Be Loved and Accepted At All Costs.

Self-respect means that you hold a good amount of love and respect for yourself. When people do not feel loved by themselves, they will tend to seek out this love from other people, no matter what it takes. This often involves putting their needs and wants to the side in order to feel loved or appreciated in return. This is harmful as it is a way of showing yourself that you are not worthy of having your own needs met. If you can work on your self-respect, you will naturally feel more secure in your relationships. What you see in yourself, others probably see in you too. If they don't, you will not need to prove it to them.

1. You Become Frazzled Or Flustered.

Often while communicating, especially in times of conflict, people will become flustered or frazzled. This state of mind, they are unable to communicate their needs assertively. Without clear and direct communication, both parties become frustrated. They will likely begin communicating in a way that involves some or all of the following:

- Shaming

- Threatening

- Judging
- Coercing
- Blaming
- Accusing
- Ridiculing
- Criticizing
- Demanding
- Labeling

THEN ONE OR BOTH PARTIES will shut down. For this reason, they have trouble having their needs met, and their conversation usually does not result in any sort of positive resolution.

1. You Feel Insecure About Your Abilities.

Everybody has at least a handful of things that they don't like about themselves. A problem arises, however, when a person lets these insecurities take over. At this point they are unable to be assertive because of their unchecked irrational beliefs. This can include approval, sense of helplessness over change (my past determines my future), anxious and ruminating thoughts etc.

---

1. You Have A Fear Of Retaliation

PEOPLE OFTEN LIE TO themselves because they are not strong enough to admit insecurity and vulnerability. Many people try their very best to avoid confrontations with other people, whether they want to admit this fact or not. It all comes down to simply not being ready to speak up for themselves due to the fear of retaliation or confrontation. If you have trouble communicating in an assertive way, this may be the reason why.

---

1. You Are Afraid That People Will Think Badly Of You Or Judge You

IF YOU OFTEN THOUGHT you were being judged by others, you may have a deep-seated fear of being judged. For this reason, you may be afraid to speak up about your needs or wants. Think about your past, does this sound like you? If so, now that you recognize this, you can begin to practice non-judgment of your own thoughts, emotions, and behaviors. Thi will make it easier to practice self-care and speak up for yourself despite your fears of judgment.

---

1. You Are Accustomed to Being Criticized By Those Who Play An Important Role In Your Life.

EVERYTHING WE SEE AS children, we are observing in order to learn more about people, the world, and how to interact with it. The impact that parental modeling has on children's development and future is not to be underestimated. If you have ever wondered why you have feelings of low self-confidence or self-esteem, think back on what was modeled for you as a child. Maybe you were ridiculed or shamed when you spoke up or shared your opinion. Maybe you also saw your parents doing this to each other in their interactions. As a result of this, you learned to think that your opinions, ideas, or needs are unimportant. What you saw and learned as a child does not determine your future. It is never too late to learn how to become more assertive. Understanding where your challenges began is the first step, not a life sentence. Becoming more assertive has the potential to change your life and your relationships.

---

1. You Fear "Saying the Wrong Thing."

SOME PEOPLE ARE AFRAID to say the wrong thing when they are with others. They are afraid of saying or doing something that may hurt or upset the other person. This can often lead a person to become quite concerned with everything that comes out of their mouth. As a result, they use passive or passive aggressive communication. This ends in miscommunication and unmet needs all around.

One very important thing to note here is that there are many ways to share your perspective. There is not one single perfect way to express yourself, but there are effective ways to express yourself in order to meet your needs. The real question is not 'what is the right thing to say' but 'how can I express my point of view most effectively'.

---

1. You Fear Hurting or Offending Others

THIS FEAR IS A CONTINUATION from the previous example, where a person has a fear of saying the wrong thing and hurting people. For this reason, a person may choose not to communicate at all. That is, unless it is in agreement with the other people they are interacting with. As in the earlier example of a person with crumbs on his shirt, the person may not be happy with what you have to say but they may need to hear it.

1. You Fear Others Will Discover How Little You Know

THIS FEAR IS ROOTED in a lack of self-confidence. As I have mentioned throughout this book, a lack of self-confidence is a large contributing factor to having struggles with assertiveness. Some people may have trouble communicating assertively because they have a fear of other people thinking that they are an impostor or that they are making things up. If you have a lack of confidence, this is a common fear. In order to combat this roadblock to assertiveness, we must first address the low level of self-confidence that comes with it.

1. You Fear Being Challenged

THIS IS YET ANOTHER fear that is associated with a low level of self-confidence. If you are not confident in yourself and your abilities, you will likely have a great fear of being challenged. You may worry that you will not know how to respond to being challenged. Those with confidence in the face of challenge, still feel fear but face the challenge anyway. In order to develop self-confidence, you will need to start facing rather than avoiding these challenges. With practice, you can feel secure, even if you are challenged because you have the experience to back it up. You will believe in what you are saying and doing. You won't spend time dwelling on whether you think other people think it is true or not. You can be confident in just asking for it. What other people say is an opportunity to get more information or experience.

Communication Blockers

The final obstacle to assertive communication is something called a "communication blocker." A communication blocker is an action that leads to a breakdown in communication and, often, a conflict. Many people use communication blockers as a reaction to a situation or conversation in which they do not feel heard, understood, or valued. Below, I will outline the nine most common communication blockers.

1. Accusations

Many people begin by accusing the other person in the interaction. This is done for various reasons, including feeling threatened or attempting to force the other person to back down.

1. Sarcasm

Have you ever met someone who approaches every situation with sarcasm, no matter how serious the matter? This is another common communication blocker because it leads people to feel disrespected and shut down.

1. Threats or Ultimatums

Threatening others can lead to a complete communication breakdown because it leads people to shut down and refuse to engage any further. It leads to power imbalances and is disrespectful.

1. Interrupting

Interrupting is a sign of disrespect and shows others that you feel your words or ideas are more important than theirs. This will not lead to a collaborative or honest discussion.

1. Judging

Sometimes, people will judge others in an interaction without getting to know them properly first. Judging leads to misunderstandings and causes people to feel ignored or insecure. This usually happens when the person is particularly critical of themselves.

1. Insulting

This one is very common, especially in an emotionally-charged situation. People often resort to insulting others to divert attention or make the other person feel inferior.

1. Always/Never statements

Using these statements is dismissive and invalidating because it is an oversimplification. When you do this, it seems like you aren't really listening to understand. Instead, try to listen and learn from others without globalizing.

1. Fact-Checking

It is socially unacceptable to immediately ask other people in the room about a speaker's statements, leading to communication breakdown. While I don't advocate for blindly believing what everyone says, there is a way to check the facts AND increase communication. A better approach is to respectfully explore the person's statements with clarifying questions. This leads to greater understanding for all parties.

1. Avoidance (changing the subject)

By changing the subject of conversation abruptly, other people think that you either don't understand or you are not interested in what they have to share.

Recap and Action Items

In this chapter, we learned about the various obstacles you may face when communicating assertively.

As you'll notice, many of the obstacles in this chapter relate to fears that you may have. Try to think about which of these fears are relevant to you and how you can begin to combat them. Next, try to determine which communication blockers you use in your life and some reasons why you may feel the need to use them.

Chapter 9: What Should You Do When You Slip up?

When learning something new, everybody experiences slip-ups. Not to worry, this chapter will teach you what to do when you accidentally resort to your old communication style.

How to Approach a Slip-Up

Let's talk about how to approach the challenges you will likely face when trying to incorporate a new communication style into your life.

We already know that hardship and failure are a necessary part of life. The cost of making any change in your life is the struggle that comes with setbacks. The good news is that understanding the challenges that you may face will help you prepare for these obstacles ahead of time. Put a plan in place that you can turn to when challenges present themselves. This can help you productively deal with them, rather allowing them to negatively affect your progress, and returning to old habits.

An example of a plan is keeping a meditation app or feel good playlist on your phone that you can turn to in the event that you feel emotional distress. Using this app will allow you to interrupt your emotional spiral long enough to make different choices.

One important takeaway that I want you to remember is that failures are necessary when you begin trying to incorporate a new habit into your life. Failures are experience, and experience is necessary for change. Do not begin your journey of developing a new habit thinking that you aren't going to fail. That is only going to discourage you from picking yourself back up. Failures are opportunities to learn!

How to Move Forward

Consistency is the key when you are looking to improve something in your mind. Consistency is the act of performing a task or an action repeatedly over a period of time. This act builds habit and experience.

A person's brain engrains habits in neural pathways in our brain that become more ingrained over time. If you have been using one communication style for your entire life, you must understand that changing this will be a process. Although that sounds daunting, I promise you it will get easier the more consistent you are with it.

By being consistent with your mindfulness and exercising the many techniques you learned, you will get better at using assertive communication. When you prioritize consistency over perfection, you will find that you are more successful at developing new habits and breaking free from the old ones.

Once your helpful habits are deeply ingrained, you won't even have to think about them anymore. That's the level that I want you to reach.

Consistency is necessary for success when making changes in your life. Therefore, to begin using assertive communication in every interaction you have, you must remain consistent in practicing it, no matter how many times you slip-up.

Tips

First, prioritize consistency over everything. It's going to be messy, you win when you show up! You do not want to beat yourself up during this process. This will only discourage you and falsely lower your confidence, making it harder to be assertive. Cultivating a growth mindset will allow you to remain motivated when things are difficult.

Everybody's objective for change will differ slightly and will likely be quite personal. Whatever your objective, writing it down will help to solidify it and make it real. Then, when you are feeling discouraged or scared, you can remind yourself of why you began in the first place. When it comes to mindset, being aware of your motivation is extremely beneficial.

Recap and Action Items

Make an action plan for the next time you slip up. Then, if you do, read it over, and you can move forward confidently.

Chapter 10: Assertive Communication for Different Settings

This chapter will look at real-world examples of assertive communication. We will examine different situations, from familial relationships to workplace discussions.

Social

There is not only one definition of what a friendship constitutes or doesn't constitute. However, these are the most common traits of friendship:

- Both people have a desire for regular contact with one another

- There is some degree of commitment, whether it's to the friendship itself or to both people's well-being

- There is mutual trust, compassion, and concern

- These two people may share common hobbies, interests, beliefs, and opinions

- These two people share knowledge about one another's interests, loves, fears, or emotions

- These two people both share feels of respect, love, appreciation, or admiration for each other

The points above indicate that for a friendship to be healthy and respectful, both people feel trust, concern, an understanding of beliefs, respect, and so on. This means that in order for you to have and maintain a healthy friendship, you must be assertive when it comes to your beliefs, needs, interests, etc. This will allow your friend to respect and account for your wants and needs.

Familial

Family does not have to be blood related but that is the common perception. To help you understand even further what being assertive means, I will provide you with a familial example.

Imagine if your mother wanted you to come over to her house as soon as possible so you can help her pack up her things to prepare for a move. However, you had planned to spend your evening relaxing, because you have had a busy week at work. Assertiveness, in this case, would be valuing your own needs just as much as you value your mother's needs. A person who respects themselves will be able to demonstrate assertiveness by saying, "I need to relax and take care of myself tonight. I will be able to enjoy helping mom tomorrow with a clear mind." Somebody with low self-respect will typically think, "It will be selfish of me to take a break when somebody needs my help." A part of having self-respect is being able to understand that you can't pour from an empty glass. In the example above, those with low self-respect will go and help their mother move right away. They will likely be exhausted and end up feeling disrespected and resentful toward their mother. In reality, people do not know what you need if you are unable to communicate it. You are really the one that disrespected yourself.

Parent and Parent

Having a healthy and respectful relationship between two parents is important for the parents themselves, as well as for the children. By having a healthy marriage or partnership, the parents are able to thoughtfully and respectfully join forces to parent effectively and raise emotionally healthy children.

If you are a parent, you have taken the first step in parenting your kids in the best way possible by reading this book.

Parent and Child

The relationship between a child and a parent can be hard to navigate, as you must find a balance between discipline and TLC. This is where assertiveness comes in. Speaking to your children aggressively will only make them fear you, which is not what you want as a parent. Instead, you want them to respect you. On the other hand, they will not respect you if you allow them to walk all over you. By practicing assertive communication with your children, they will respect you and the boundaries that you set for them.

For example, if you want your child to remain in their bedroom after you put them to bed, you do not want to aggressively yell at them, passive aggressively suggest, nor do you want to passively ask them to follow this rule. Instead, you want to assertively tell them your expectation and the consequences if they choose not to follow. Consequences should be clear, appropriate, and progressive. There's no reason for consequences to be emotionally charged, they are direct reflections of actions as in life.

Parents model everything for their children, and this is where kids learn and discover everything about life and conducting themselves. Suppose a child always experiences violent communication in the home, and no other type of communication is modeled for them. They may grow into an adult unaware of any other type of communication style. Children may learn to judge others and shame them in order to meet their needs. They may also feel judged and shamed, and this could lead to depression. Modeling passive aggressive communication leaves children feeling confused and unstable. The parents' actions don't match their words and this incongruence is upsetting and the children may not even understand why. Modeling passive communication leaves children undisciplined. Children who have friends as parents lack discipline and struggle to problem solve, as they don't experience consequences growing up. When they are told no as an adult they do not know how to regulate their emotions and deal with disappointment.

Romantic Relationships

Being assertive involves mutual respect with your partner and letting each other know when you are not feeling respected. This comes in the form of boundaries, as we discussed earlier in this book.

When a relationship is healthy, the people in the relationship prioritize hard conversations. Talking about a problem rather than holding it in comes naturally with time and practice. This allows them both to get what they need from the relationship. Having the courage to practice honest and open communication is crucial when it comes to having a healthy relationship. The first step is to make sure both people understand and express their needs and expectations to each other.

Employer and Employee

We will now look at an example of assertiveness, this time in the workplace between a boss and their employee.

Imagine your boss just asked you for the third time this month to do your co-worker's report because he has fallen behind schedule again. Your boss is asking you because she knows that you work more efficiently than your coworker.

A person with self-respect who is comfortable with assertive communication will be able to respond,

"This is the third time in a month that I have received extra work because John is behind schedule. I value being a team player, but I feel stressed when I am overwhelmed. This is my workload and I will not be able to finish both. How would you like me to prioritize?"

The above example is the correct way to respond assertively in a situation like this because you are demonstrating that you respect yourself and are saying, "enough is enough." Your responsibility is to inform your boss what you are capable of doing in the time allotted and it's your boss's responsibility to distribute the load and prioritize appropriately. Be firm with what you can do and allow the leader to decide which tasks are most important, which can be pushed off, and which can be given to someone else.

Typically, in this situation, a person with low self-confidence would agree to take on the extra work and end up resenting their boss for it. They end up suffering in silence, draining themselves by doing extra work and blaming other people for their struggles. By avoiding hard conversations, they create toxic relationships and build resentment. The moral of this story is: letting people know how you feel and what you need gives them the chance to adjust accordingly.

Introverts and Extroverts

Introverts and extroverts communicate using a variety of styles. Most often introverts are agreeable and tagged as passive or passive aggressive communicators. While extroverts who regularly practice verbal processing are pegged as aggressive or assertive communicators. These assumptions are not only unfair to both introverts and extroverts but they are not necessarily correct. Introverts and extroverts are equally able to develop assertive communication skills.

Passive communicators are not often treated very well because they have a difficult time expressing themselves clearly enough that others

CAN treat them well. If you are too passive, you risk constant miscommunication and appearing incompetent as you don't clarify or express your own ideas. Conversely, aggressive communicators are often able to get what they want, but in the process, lack connection with others as they ignore the human element to work (feeling). If you are too aggressive, you risk looking unprofessional and volatile. The happy medium is assertiveness.

If you are an introvert, you probably avoid all situations that could potentially lead to a conflict. In contrast, if you are an extrovert, you stare confrontation in the face and maybe even initiate it. The key is to find a balance between these two extremes, regardless of whether you are extroverted or introverted. Either type of person has the ability to be assertive.

Recap and Action Items

In this chapter, you learned about assertive communication in different scenarios. Try to break each of these sections into more specific scenarios and come up with your own examples for how to use assertive communication in that scenario. For example, an extrovert in conflict with their spouse. How should they approach this situation from the perspective of assertive communication? Come up with as many examples as you can and try to think of the best approach from the lens of assertive communication.

Chapter 11: Sample Scripts for Assertive Communication

In this final chapter, you will find some sample scripts that will help you understand assertive communication on a deeper level by seeing examples in practice.

At Work

Practicing assertive communication in a work setting can be challenging. It requires sharing your perspective, setting boundaries, and asking for what you need. When setting a boundary, it becomes clear who is responsible for which task. It is possible to value quality work AND allow a piece of the project (the piece that is not your responsibility) to fail.

This is often where people have a hard time holding boundaries. You see the deadline approaching and your coworker is not holding up their end. To save the project, you begrudgingly take on their load as well as yours. When it comes time to present the project everyone gets credit and you silently stew in bitterness. Your stress builds as the projects continue in the same way until you unintentionally snap at your coworker, or even worse your boss and get reprimanded.

With assertive communication, tasks are divided clearly and appropriately. If coworkers choose to not complete their part of the project, don't rescue them from their responsibilities and consequences. Actions change when there are direct consequences, you getting pissed and resentful is not a significant enough consequence...just an annoyance.

The reality is: Your irritation is your problem, not theirs.

Example

You are at work, and a co-worker of yours has been consistently neglecting their work. They have been going on social media all day instead of doing their tasks. You have been picking up the extra work. You have a deadline coming up, so you cannot refuse to do the extra work. This has been frustrating you for some time, and today it has come to a head. Your boss has been yelling at you today because the team is behind on their targets. You are about to lose it due to anger.

Method #1: Aggressive Communication.

"You haven't been doing any work this week, I've seen you on Facebook every day and our deadline is fast approaching! I am sick of picking up after you because clearly you don't care at all. If you don't start doing your part, I'm going to talk to the boss about you."

Passive aggressive

"What's going on with Facebook? Better yet, what's going on with our project lol."

Passive

"I just got yelled at by the boss because our project is behind. Do you want me to do your part too?"

Method #2: Assertive Communication/Setting a Boundary

"Our deadline is tomorrow, and the boss noted we are behind on *these targets*. Our tasks are divided *in this manner (be specific)*. Please prioritize *these tasks* and I will prioritize *these tasks*."

Uncomfortable truth:

You are making their laziness your problem by not setting boundaries and speaking assertively.

At Home:

In some at home relationships there is a power dynamic that changes the way you interact. For example, while you would speak to everyone with respect, you would not speak to your spouse the same way you speak to your child. Your child needs you to establish and enforce boundaries which can include discipline. Your partner expects you to communicate boundaries so you can collaboratively identify and solve problems.

Roommates and friendships are a bit of a hybrid of the work and home examples.

Most situations are best addressed directly when they happen. However, when the situation requires brainstorming, collaborative problem solving and discussion, be mindful of what is going on with the other person (empathy). It is helpful to schedule a time to discuss and problem solve together. Invite input and be open to compromise, if appropriate.

Example 1

Your roommate leaves his dirty dishes all over the house, and you have been keeping quiet about it, until one day he has friends over for dinner and leaves all of the plates and cutlery in the kitchen dirty and on the table. You come home from work, hungry and tired, and want to make yourself some food, but you see that everything in the kitchen is dirty. You feel like you have had enough and finally want to say something. There are two different ways that this confrontation could go.

Method #1: Aggressive Communication. What NOT to do.

"I'm so fed up with the fact that you never do your dishes! I always clean mine but now you have used everything in the kitchen and haven't done your dishes for a week and everything is dirty! Clean up after yourself, you're a slob. You're lazy and I can't live with it anymore."

Passive aggressive

"Wow! Great job with the dishes. I guess I'll just eat with my hands. I am starving but I'm glad you had friends over to use all of our dishes!"

Passive

"Are there any other dishes that need to be cleaned? I'm washing them now."

Method #2: Assertive Communication

"I was going to make dinner but all the dishes and silverware are dirty. I'm frustrated because I keep things clean for comfort and convenience. Please clean up after your guests and I'll do the same."

At Home: Example 2

Deciding who is going to take your dog for a walk.

Method #1: Aggressive Communication. What NOT to do.

"You never walk the dog! When will you finally pull your weight in this house?"

Passive aggressive

"Did you walk the dog? I mean, it would be nice if you walked the dog once in a while. I guess I'll just do it every time since you're *so* busy."

Passive

"I took the dog out. I'm so tired."

Method #2: Assertive Communication

"I feel anxious when I walk the dog in the evening because it's so late. I prefer to go to bed early. I am happy to take him for a morning walk though. I'd like to hear your suggestions too."

At Home: Example 3

Your child needs to do their homework, and you are getting frustrated that they have not done it yet.

Method #1: Aggressive Communication. What NOT to do.

"Stop being so lazy and get your homework done; otherwise, I will throw your video game out the window!"

Passive aggressive

"I'm *so glad* you're playing video games instead of doing your homework. That's *really* going to help you succeed in life."

Passive

"Kids will be kids."

Method #2: Assertive Communication/Setting Boundaries with (Pre-)Teenagers

"As we've discussed, you can play video games after you finish your homework. If you choose to play video games and not finish your homework, you will not be able to play until I see evidence homework is complete. If this continues to be an issue, we will renegotiate your access to video games."

Note: Parenting is difficult. Avoid reacting (or overreacting). Be firm. Be Clear. Be Assertive.

At Public

The relationship between classmates is a unique one. This is because you spend so much of your time with classmates, sometimes even more than with your own family. However, in most cases, you would not share your deepest feelings or thoughts. Depending on what type of school you go to, the relationships between classmates can become very competitive and cut-throat. It is very difficult to use assertive communication in this type of situation, as you may risk being judged or shamed in a moment of emotional vulnerability.

Sometimes there will be conflicts between classmates, and the way that these are dealt with says a lot about the people involved and the workplace itself. By approaching these conflicts using assertive communication, the people involved have the potential to develop a deeper understanding of one another and even if they are not friends, understanding the needs of others is an important part of having a mutually respectful relationship.

For example, a classmate comes up to you and asks you what grade you received on the test. You do not feel comfortable telling them, in fear of being made fun of.

Method #1: Aggressive Communication. What NOT to do.

"I'm not telling you, it's none of your business and you're so nosy!"

Passive Aggressive

"So I guess I'm telling everyone my grades now. I might as well shout it from the rooftops since it's anyone's business."

Passive

"Umm I got .."

Method #2: Assertive Communication

I am not comfortable sharing that information, please don't ask me again.

Note: The classmate may continue to push. Be Consistent. Be Firm.

Recap and Action Items

Any of the example situations above have the potential to turn into a larger conflict. By using assertive communication, you can often prevent this and diffuse the situation before it becomes any sort of conflict. Using assertive communication for problem-solving is a way to discuss matters calmly and make decisions that benefit everyone involved.

Try to come up with some example scenarios for the two environments listed below. Come up with what not to do and what you should do from the perspective of assertive communication.

Conclusion

In the beginning of this book we defined communication and more importantly assertive communication. We also went over who this information would help and who it would not. In chapter 1 we discussed all the myths and misconceptions of assertive communication style. We debunked the assumptions that assertive communication is synonymous with aggressive communication.

In chapter 2 we identified the benefits of assertive communication, showing assertive communication has a relationship with self-confidence and self worth. In chapter 3 we discussed the other communication styles such as interpersonal communication, one on one and in small groups, and also public communication. Moreover, we discussed nonverbal communication such as vocal dynamics and body language. In this chapter we also identified the difference between aggressive, passive and passive aggressive communication styles as they relate with assertive communication. We were also very clear about the difference between being nice and being kind.

In chapter 4 we talked about specific assertive communication skills such as self-awareness and self-evaluation by determining your current communication style, and we also evaluated how assertive you actually are. We discussed empathy and sympathy. We also covered the benefits of empathy, active listening and how to use empathetic dialogue while being assertive.

Chapter 5 was all about setting boundaries. First we defined boundaries then we discussed the importance of setting them. After that we talked about how to actually do it by speaking up, commanding respect and being consistent. Moreover we discussed how to figure out your feelings by noticing sensations in your body, giving your feelings a name, and going deeper into that thought process.

In chapter 6 we introduced how to communicate and emotional state. First we talked about why it's important to not communicate when you're emotionally charged. Then we discussed the benefits of calming yourself so that you're able to really listen to the other person. We also went over strategies for calming yourself such as writing your feelings down and trying to laugh. Don't forget mindfulness is very important when it comes to communicating your emotional state.

In chapter 8 we covered the traps that you might fall into such as not knowing what you want or thinking that your needs don't matter. When we got to chapter 9 we covered what you should do when you slip up. In chapter 10 we went over assertive communication in different settings such as social, familial, parent to parent, parent to child, romantic relationships etc.... Then in chapter 11 I provided you several sample scripts for different settings you might need.

At this point you have been given all the tools and information you need to start making big changes in your life and in your communication style. If you have not already done so, go back and do all of the action steps that were at the end of each chapter. None of this works unless you take action and do the things that were discussed. With that said I wish you all the best in your future endeavors and look forward to seeing you again in another book.

If you enjoyed this book, I'd love for you to share your thoughts and post a quick review on the platform that you purchased it on.

Thank You From Story Ninjas

Story Ninjas Publishing would like to thank you for reading our book. We hope you found value in this product and would love to hear your feedback. Please provide your constructive criticism in review on the platform that you purchased it on. Also feel free to share this book through the various social media platforms.

Other Books by Story Ninjas

Story Ninjas Publishing hopes you enjoyed this book. You can check out our other books here.

About Story Ninjas

STORY NINJAS PUBLISHING is an independent book publisher. Our stories range from science fiction to paranormal romance. Our goal is to create stories that are not only entertaining, but endearing. We believe engaging narrative can lead to personal growth. Through unforgettable characters and powerful plot we portray themes that are relevant for today's issues.

You can find more Story Ninja's products here[1].

Follow Story Ninjas!!!

E-mail: Story-ninjas@story-ninjas.com

Youtube: @StoryNinjas[2]

Facebook: StoryNinjasHQ[3]

---

1. http://www.story-ninjas.com
2. https://www.youtube.com/channel/UCzoBgY53hBp8fP9tt36Krwg

3. https://www.facebook.com/storyninjashq/

About The Author

Natalie white is a life coach and communication enthusiast. She has a masters degree in psychology and has spent most of her life studying the interdynamics of people. In her free time she likes to eat chocolate ice cream and read memes on social media.

Don't miss out!

Visit the website below and you can sign up to receive emails whenever Natalie White publishes a new book. There's no charge and no obligation.

https://books2read.com/r/B-A-MUBP-PDMPB

BOOKS 2 READ

Connecting independent readers to independent writers.

Did you love *Assertive & Kind*? Then you should read *Fasting For The Carnivore Diet: The Ultimate Guide To Melting Fat And Getting Shredded While Eating Animal Based Foods*[1] by Joe Bell and Mark Rogan!

How to get shredded without exercising, even if you've tried all of the other diets out there.

When you buy this book, you'll get the following:- What is the carnivore diet- What is fasting- The problem with most diets- Who shouldn't try fasting- Background and science of fasting and eating animal-based foods- Myths and misconceptions about fasting- The countless health benefits of fasting- What is autophagy and how is it related to fasting- Your first month of fasting- How to start fasting- What to do when you mess up**Below is a short excerpt:** Fasting has been something prescribed and written about from people as early as Hip-

---

1. https://books2read.com/u/mv7dX2

2. https://books2read.com/u/mv7dX2

pocrates, who is coined the Father of Modern Medicine. He wrote that "To eat when you are sick is to feed your illness." It explains the body's natural tendency to be unable to eat when you are sick and how you feel like you've lost your appetite, or your taste buds have changed. Doctors in Greek society often prescribed fasting for patients who were sick. Great thinkers like Plato and Aristotle were also fans of fasting and feared overeating or consuming food in excess. As medicine evolved in the West, Philip Paracelsus also labeled fasting as the "physician within." He was another doctor who was considered one of the fathers of Western medicine along with Galen and Hippocrates. Even Benjamin Franklin wrote, "The best of all medicines is resting and fasting." Great thinkers of the time thought of fasting as a healing technique to aid speedy recovery and that it was always best to limit excess intake of food.Fasting, coupled with the Carnivore Diet is a simple program that requires little to no effort. Just set it an forget it. And in no time at all, you'll melt fat and get shredded.Fasting For The Carnivore Diet breaks this down into easy to follow steps, that will get you results in as little as three days. When you buy this book, you won't be able to put it down.

But don't take our word for it. Scroll up and BUY YOUR COPY TODAY!

Also by Natalie White

Assertive & Kind

About the Publisher

Story Ninjas Publishing is an independent book publisher with fiction stories that range from science fiction to romance. Our goal is to create stories that are not only entertaining, but endearing. We believe engaging narrative can lead to personal growth. Through unforgettable characters and powerful plot we portray themes that are relevant for today's issues. Our hope is that readers find lessons they can apply to their everyday lives, so that the stories live on through the actions of each person they touch. Additionally, we provide creative non-fiction books that are meant to serve as tools to help people solve everyday problems. We hope you find our products entertaining and helpful.

Printed in Dunstable, United Kingdom